kitchen wisdom

kitchen wisdom

hundreds of hints and tips for every cook

Anne Sheasby

RYLAND
PETERS
& SMALL

LONDON NEW YORK

First published in the
United States in 2007 by
Ryland Peters & Small
519 Broadway, 5th Floor
New York, NY 10012
www.rylandpeters.com

10 9 8 7 6 5 4 3 2 1

Text, design, and photographs
copyright © Ryland Peters &
Small 2007

ISBN-10: 1-84597-481-6
ISBN-13: 978-1-84597-481-7

Printed and bound in China.

Library of Congress Cataloging-
in-Publication Data

Sheasby, Anne.
  Kitchen wisdom : hundreds of
hints and tips for every cook /
Anne Sheasby.
      p. cm.
  Includes index.
  ISBN 978-1-84597-481-7
  1. Cookery. I. Title.
  TX651.S463 2007
  641.5--dc22

                    2007015914

The publisher and author cannot
accept responsibility for problems
that may arise as a result of
following the advice in this book.

For Robbie

Senior Editor
Clare Double

Picture Research
Emily Westlake

Production
Gordana Simakovic

Publishing Director
Alison Starling

U.S. Consultant
Sue Stuck

contents

staples

storage solutions

If possible, store foods on narrow shelves so that you can easily see and reach items.

CLEVER SOLUTION: If you are short of space in the kitchen, cover the sink with a piece of wood cut to size or a large chopping board to create an extra work surface when the sink is not in use.

CLEVER SOLUTION: If you don't have a spice rack, put jars of herbs and spices in a rectangular basket or plastic box for easy access. Many spice jars only have the name of the contents on the side (designed to be viewed in a spice rack), so label the top of each jar as well, for easy identification.

Mount a key holder on your kitchen wall and use it to hang useful small items, such as measuring spoons, small sieves, pastry brushes, and so on, within easy reach of your work space.

SAFETY TIP: *Stick the point of sharp implements such as skewers and knives into wine corks, to protect hands when you reach into a drawer. The cork will also help to prevent the sharp edges from becoming dull.*

CLEVER SOLUTION: Sturdy kitchen tiles make good trivets for hot pans. Glue a piece of felt or cork on the back to prevent the tile from scratching your work surface.

CLEVER SOLUTION: Wine carriers or wine boxes are also useful for transporting food on a journey or picnic. Each compartment can accommodate a different food or drink.

Choose stackable containers to maximize storage space. Square or rectangular containers make better use of shelf space than round or oval containers.

Suspend a wooden or metal rail or rack from the kitchen ceiling and add large metal hooks from which to hang pots, pans, and utensils. This will free up cupboard space and work surfaces.

Use the space between two kitchen cupboard units to store baking sheets, chopping boards, trays, and similar items, to clear shelf space.

Hang a plastic shoe rack (with clear pockets) on the inside of a kitchen cupboard door, and store small items in the pockets, such as packets of herbs and spices, bouillon cubes, nuts, and gelatine.

Use a cardboard wine carrier to store boxes of foil, plastic wrap, and similar shaped cartons upright in the slots. Store under the sink or in a cupboard to save drawer space.

A vertical metal file rack or plate drainer is an ideal way to store chopping boards, baking sheets, and pizza stones. Stored this way, they take up less space and it is easier for you to find what you need.

containers

CLEVER SOLUTION: The tops of jars or bottles of food such as honey, jam, and maple syrup may become sticky, making the lid difficult to remove. To prevent this, wipe around the rim and lid with paper towel or a clean cloth (dampened in hot water) to remove any spillages, before replacing the lid. Alternatively, cover the top of the opened jar or bottle with a piece of plastic wrap before screwing on the lid. This will help prevent the lid from sticking.

To remove odors from a container that you wish to use again, fill the container with hot water, then stir in 1 tablespoon of baking powder. Let it stand overnight, then wash, rinse well, and dry before use.

If you transfer foods from packets to storage containers, Scotch tape the food label onto the container so you can easily identify its contents. Make a note of the "use-by" or "best-before" date on the container, too.

Masking tape is a great way of labeling containers. Simply stick a length of masking tape on the container and write on the tape. Fold over one end of the tape to create a tab, for easy removal. Also, every time you open a new jar or bottle, write the date on a piece of masking tape and stick it to the side of the container.

Save empty spice or herb jars with perforated lids inside. Wash and dry them thoroughly, then use them to store flour, sugar, or confectioners' sugar. When you need a little flour to dust a work surface or sugar to shake over a cake, you will have it on hand.

MONEY-SAVING IDEA: Make your own flour or sugar shaker by carefully hammering a new nail through the metal lid of a clean, screw-top jar to make several holes. Put some flour or sugar in the jar, replace the lid, and you have a shaker ready to use.

If you are having trouble opening a twist-top jar or bottle, grip the lid wearing a rubber glove, or use a rubber band or damp cloth instead. Alternatively, hold the lid under hot running water—the heat should expand the metal and make opening easier. Use a pair of nutcrackers to carefully grip and loosen small lids.

STORAGE TIP: *Store flour in its original sealed packaging or in an airtight container in a cool, dry, airy place. Ideally, buy and store small quantities at a time, to help avoid infestation of psocids (very small, barely visible, gray-brown insects) or pantry moths, which may appear in the cleanest homes. If you do find these small insects in your flour, dispose of it immediately and wash and dry the container thoroughly. Never mix new flour with old.*

food basics & taste tips

If you run out of self-rising flour, sift together 1 level tablespoon of baking powder with every 2½ cups all-purpose flour. This will not create quite such a high lift as self-rising flour, but it makes a good substitute.

TASTE TIP: *Use freshly brewed tea to add flavor and color to sweet and savory dishes such as meat casseroles and ice creams (using scented teas), and as the basis for fruit punches. Brewed tea can also be used to soak dried fruits for compotes, or for use in rich fruit cakes or fruit loaves.*

Some raw fruits including pineapple, kiwi, and papaya contain an enzyme that prevents gelatine from setting. However, they can be used in gelatine-set recipes if they are cooked first, as cooking destroys the enzyme.

TASTE TIP: *Choose a reasonable quality wine for cooking, especially if the wine is not going to be heated, as in a fruit salad or syllabub. Cooking will not improve a wine that tastes off or is inferior in flavor. Port or sherry can add extra flavor and color to casseroles, soups, sauces, fruit cakes, compotes, and other dishes.*

Gelatine is commonly available as powder. Follow the package instructions carefully for use. As a guide to quantities, 1 sachet of powdered gelatine will set 2 cups of liquid.

Avoid adding hot gelatine liquid to cold mixtures, otherwise it will set on contact and form fine threads or lumps. Always add dissolved gelatine to a mixture that is warm or at room temperature.

Alcohol reduces the setting power of gelatine. If you use wine in a gelatine-set recipe, heat it so the alcohol evaporates before you add the gelatine.

SAFETY TIP: *Leftover canned foods should be transferred to an airtight container, kept in the refrigerator, and eaten within 2 days. Once cans are opened, the contents should be treated as fresh food. This doesn't apply to ingredients sold in cans with resealable lids, such as cocoa powder.*

TASTE TIP: *To add flavor to dried stuffing mix, add some chopped dried fruit, chopped nuts, lightly toasted seeds, or finely grated fresh Parmesan cheese before use.*

To test the freshness of baking powder, mix 2 teaspoons with 1 cup hot tap water. If there is an immediate fizzing and foaming reaction, the baking powder can be used. If there is little or no reaction or a delayed reaction, discard the baking powder.

TECHNIQUE TIP: *If you don't have a pizza cutter, cut a baked pizza into slices with clean kitchen scissors.*

STORAGE TIP:
Store coffee (beans and ground) in the refrigerator or freezer, or it will go stale very quickly.

flavorings

herbs

STORAGE TIP: *Store all dried herbs and spices in a cool, dark, dry place. Spice racks filled with glass jars, unless they are in a cupboard, are not a good idea.*

STORAGE TIP: *Store fresh herbs in the refrigerator. Wrap them loosely in an unsealed plastic food bag, or in a paper bag. Fresh herbs should keep well in the salad drawer for several days.*

The best time to pick fresh herbs for freezing or drying is just before they flower, when their flavor is at its most potent.

TECHNIQUE TIP: *To dry herbs, hang small, freshly picked bunches in a warm, dry area such as near the stove. Once dry, store the herbs in airtight containers. Use them within 4 months of drying, or while still fragrant.*

STORAGE TIP: *Chop leftover fresh herbs, spoon them into an ice-cube tray, top each portion with a little water, and freeze. Once solid, put the cubes in a freezer bag. Seal, label, and return to the freezer. Add the frozen herb cubes to soups, casseroles, and sauces as needed.*

CLEVER SOLUTION: Use a salad spinner to wash and dry fresh herbs. It saves time and helps prevent the delicate leaves from bruising.

When substituting dried herbs for fresh, use roughly half the quantity the recipe calls for, as dried herbs have a more concentrated flavor.

CLEVER SOLUTION: If a recipe calls for snipped fresh chives but you don't have any, try using finely chopped scallion instead.

TASTE TIP: *To impart a smoky herb flavor to grilled food, scatter sprigs of fresh rosemary or thyme (soaked in water first to make them last longer) over the hot coals just before cooking.*

HEALTHY HINT: *Use fresh or dried herbs or spices to improve the flavor of many dishes, without adding extra fat or salt.*

A fresh bouquet garni usually contains a couple of parsley stalks, a sprig of thyme, a bay leaf, and sometimes celery leaves and black peppercorns, tied together. To make one, either tie the herbs together with kitchen string (using bay leaves or a section of leek as the outer wrapper), or tie everything in a small piece of cheesecloth.

TECHNIQUE TIP: *When preparing fresh basil, tear the leaves rather than cutting them, as the sharp blade of a knife can easily bruise these delicate leaves.*

TASTE TIP: *Chopped fresh herb stems (such as parsley stalks) are great for adding flavor to soups, sauces, and casseroles.*

TIME-SAVING TIP: *A quick and easy way to chop fresh herbs is to use kitchen scissors to snip them directly into a bowl or over food, rather than using a sharp knife and chopping board.*

spices

If possible, buy whole, dried spices and crush them yourself, as required. Crushing your own spices ensures maximum flavor every time. Once spices are ground, they lose their flavor and deteriorate quite quickly. Spices can be ground using a pestle and mortar or in an electric coffee grinder kept specially for spices. As a general guide, replace ground spices (including those you have ground yourself) every 6 months.

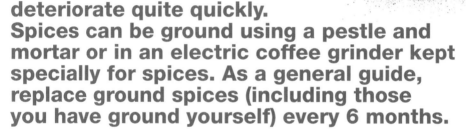

TASTE TIP: *Try mixing a pinch or two of ground spices such as curry powder, ground red pepper, or turmeric with breadcrumbs or flour, and use this to coat foods before frying. Add ground spices such as cinnamon, apple pie spice, or ginger to fruit crumble toppings. A few gratings of fresh nutmeg will perk up mashed potatoes, cheese sauce, cooked spinach, and rice or semolina puddings. A little ground allspice will add flavor to mashed root vegetables such as rutabagas or parsnips.*

TASTE TIP: *When making a goulash, try using smoked paprika instead of ordinary paprika. Smoked paprika will add a gentle heat and spiciness to the dish.*

The color of a fresh chile is no indication of how hot it will be. Most chiles are green when they are immature, ripening to varying shades of red. Generally speaking, the smaller and thinner the chile, the hotter it will be.

SAFETY TIP: *The natural oils in chiles may cause irritation to your skin and eyes. When preparing them, wear disposable gloves or pull a small plastic bag over each hand, secured with an elastic band around the wrist, to create a glove.*

Which is hottest—ground red pepper, cayenne pepper, or paprika? Ground red pepper and cayenne pepper are made from finely ground dried capsicums. Both are hot, but cayenne tends to be a little hotter. Paprika is made from ground dried sweet red peppers and is generally milder and sweet in flavor. There are several types, including Hungarian paprika, which is hotter than Spanish paprika. Paprika from the USA tends to be mild.

TASTE TIP: *To reduce the heat of a fresh chile, cut it in half lengthways, then scrape out and discard the seeds and membranes (or core).*

TECHNIQUE TIP: *To make chile pepper rings for garnishing, cut the stem end off a fresh pepper, then insert a swivel vegetable peeler and rotate it inside to loosen the seeds and membranes. Shake any remaining seeds out of the chile, then slice it thinly into rings.*

TECHNIQUE TIP: *Use a melon baller to prepare fresh chiles. Cut the chile in half lengthways then, using the edge of a melon baller, scrape down the inside of each half, removing the seeds and membranes as you go. Alternatively, use a small spoon or sharp knife instead of a melon baller.*

other flavorings

When buying garlic, choose plump bulbs with tightly packed cloves and dry skin. Avoid soft, moldy, shriveled, or sprouting garlic.

TECHNIQUE TIP: *An easy way to prepare fresh garlic is to grate peeled whole cloves on a fine grater. This will produce finely chopped garlic ready for use.*

CLEVER SOLUTION: Use a new, clean toothbrush to clean all the little holes in a garlic press, and to scrape off lemon zest caught in the teeth of the grater.

TASTE TIP: *If you plan to freeze a recipe containing garlic, it is best to cook the dish without garlic, then add it to the food after thawing. Garlic can taste musty when frozen.*

If you have leftover fresh ginger, cut it into thick slices and freeze in a freezer bag for up to 1 month. Defrost, peel, and slice, chop, or grate as required.

SAFETY TIP: *To grate fresh ginger easily, peel a small portion at one end of a large piece then grate that portion, using the unpeeled length of ginger as a handle.*

TECHNIQUE TIP: *Use a garlic press to extract juice from small pieces of fresh ginger. Use the ginger juice in salad dressings and sauces.*

If a recipe calls for fresh ginger, do not use dried (ground) ginger instead, and vice versa—the flavors are very different.

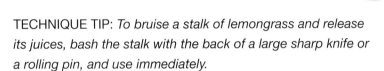

TECHNIQUE TIP: *To crush black peppercorns coarsely, spread an even layer in a plastic bag. Seal the bag, dispelling the air inside, then bash the peppercorns with a rolling pin or meat tenderizer.*

TECHNIQUE TIP: *To bruise a stalk of lemongrass and release its juices, bash the stalk with the back of a large sharp knife or a rolling pin, and use immediately.*

TASTE TIP: *Stir whole-grain mustard into mashed potatoes or mayonnaise before serving to add extra flavor. Mustard also enhances salad dressings and sauces. A pinch of powdered mustard added to cheese dishes will enhance the flavor.*

TASTE TIP: *Combine a little flour and powdered mustard, season with salt and pepper, then rub over a joint of beef before roasting, to add delicious flavor.*

Rescue Remedy: **If you add too much salt to a soup or casserole, add one or two peeled potatoes (cut into chunks) to soak up the salt, cooking them until tender. Discard the potatoes before serving.**

TECHNIQUE TIP: *To remove the edible seeds from a vanilla bean, use a small sharp knife to cut the bean in half lengthways. Starting at one end of each piece, press the knife down to scrape out the seeds, flattening the bean as you go. The empty bean can also be used as a flavoring in a sauce or added to sugar.*

Pure vanilla extract is an alcoholic extract of the vanilla bean. The much cheaper imitation vanilla has an aggressive artificial flavor.

oils

STORAGE TIP: *Store oils, well sealed, in a cool, dark, dry place, away from direct sunlight. They can be kept in the fridge (though this is not necessary), but oils such as olive oil tend to solidify and go cloudy in the fridge. If this happens, bring the oil back to room temperature before use.*

Buy oil in small bottles as it can become rancid if kept too long. Nut oils, such as walnut or hazelnut, are the most unstable, so buy them in small amounts and use them up fairly quickly after opening.

SAFETY TIP: *Never fill a deep-fat fryer more than one-third full of oil. Once the food has been added to the oil, the pan should be no more than half full.*

TECHNIQUE TIP: *Deep-fry foods in small batches and let the oil heat back up before adding the next batch. This will ensure that the food remains crisp. If too much food is deep-fried at one time, the temperature of the oil is reduced, so the outer coating will not be crispy. The food then absorbs fat and is less tasty.*

TASTE TIP: *For a richer-flavored salad dressing, use a nut oil instead of olive or plain vegetable oil.*

CLEVER SOLUTION: Oil often drips down the sides of the bottle. Make a thick cuff of kitchen paper and fasten it around the neck of the bottle with an elastic band to catch any drips. Replace as necessary.

marinades

Marinades are used to add flavor to food and keep it moist, and to have a tenderizing effect. Meat, poultry, game, fish, shellfish, and vegetables can all be marinated. The marinated food is then cooked (with the exception of a few fish dishes, such as ceviche), often by grilling or roasting. When grilling, the marinade may be basted on the food during the initial stages of cooking, or reduced and thickened separately in a pan to make an accompanying sauce.

Many marinades contain an acid ingredient such as lemon juice, vinegar, or wine, so always marinate foods in non-metallic containers. Metallic dishes may react with the acid in the marinade.

CLEVER SOLUTION: An easy way to marinate meat or poultry is to use a plastic food bag. Put the meat in the bag, add the marinade, and seal. Shake the bag, ensuring the meat is completely covered in the marinade. Once the meat is marinated, remove the meat and discard the bag. Never save and reuse marinades.

SAFETY TIP: *If using a raw meat marinade to make a sauce, make sure that the sauce is boiled before serving, to kill off any bacteria.*

Plain yogurt is sometimes used as a marinade as it contains active enzymes, which tenderize the food as well as adding flavor. One example of this is chicken tikka.

stocks, sauces, & soups

stocks

TECHNIQUE TIP: *When making stocks, use a large pan with a pasta basket into which you can put all the solid ingredients. Once the stock is cooked, simply lift out the basket, leaving behind the liquid stock. Straining it is much easier without all the solid ingredients.*

TECHNIQUE TIP: *Meat or poultry stock requires long, slow simmering so that the maximum flavor can be extracted from the bones. Fish stock is made quickly and vegetable stock can be made relatively quickly or slowly.*

CLEVER SOLUTION: To remove fat from the surface of stock, pour the stock into a pitcher and add a few ice cubes. When the fat has set around the ice, lift it off and discard.

TECHNIQUE TIP: *Boiling stock tends to make it cloudy. To make a clear, rich stock, simmer it gently over very low heat.*

When making stocks, do not include potatoes or potato peelings as they will make the stock cloudy.

TASTE TIP: *Parsley stalks are often used in stocks because they have more flavor than the leaves, and the leaves will turn bitter if cooked for a long period.*

HEALTHY HINT: *Do not add salt to homemade stock. This allows you to control the amount of salt in any dish you make with the stock. Note that many ready-made stocks are very salty.*

TASTE TIP: *Use the water in which ham has been boiled to cook green vegetables, giving them a lovely flavor. You can also use the cooking liquid as the basis for soup, if it is not too salty.*

STORAGE TIP: *It is best to reduce stock by rapid boiling to get a concentrated stock for freezing. Frozen stock can be defrosted, or reheated from frozen, and it should then be simmered for at least 10 minutes. Frozen concentrated stock can also be diluted once defrosted, if desired.*

STORAGE TIP: *Homemade stock can be frozen in handy portions for future use. Pour the cooled stock into the cups of a nonstick muffin pan and freeze until solid. Remove the frozen blocks from the muffin tin, put them in a freezer bag, seal, label, and freeze. Remove stock portions as you need them. Concentrated stock can be frozen in the same way, using ice-cube trays instead of a muffin pan.*

TASTE TIP: *When serving plain rice as an accompaniment, cook it in a well-flavored stock (meat, chicken, or vegetable, depending on the main dish) rather than in water, to add extra flavor.*

sauces

TECHNIQUE TIP: *When making emulsified sauces such as mayonnaise or Hollandaise, use a small blender or food processor to combine the ingredients. This will help prevent curdling or separation.*

When making emulsified sauces, make sure all the ingredients are at room temperature. Mayonnaise may curdle if the eggs are used straight from the fridge.

CLEVER SOLUTION: *When making an egg custard sauce such as crème anglaise, add 1 teaspoon of cornstarch to the eggs and sugar. This will help to stabilize the custard and reduce the risk of curdling. Once the sauce has thickened, cook it gently for slightly longer to remove the taste of the cornstarch.*

Fine fresh breadcrumbs can be used to thicken some sauces and casseroles. Gradually stir the breadcrumbs in towards the end of the cooking time and simmer (adding extra breadcrumbs, if desired) until you have the thickness required.

TASTE TIP: *Add a generous dash or two of sherry, Madeira, port, or red or white wine to gravy to add a rich and delicious flavor. Alternatively, stir in a little horseradish sauce, mustard, cayenne pepper, or dried or chopped fresh herbs to add a more distinct flavor to gravy.*

TASTE TIP: *To boost a chocolate sauce, add a dash or two of whisky, brandy, or rum just before serving.*

Rescue Remedy: To rescue a lumpy sauce or gravy, whisk it vigorously, using a balloon whisk, until smooth. Alternatively, pour the lumpy sauce into a small blender or food processor and blend for about 1 minute, until smooth. You can also pour the sauce or gravy through a fine sieve into a clean pan.

Rescue Remedy: **If an emulsified sauce such as Hollandaise begins to curdle, add an ice cube and whisk it thoroughly until smooth— the sauce should recombine. Similarly, if an emulsified sauce such as beurre blanc becomes too hot during preparation, it will turn greasy and split. Whisking in an ice cube should rescue it.**

RESCUE REMEDY: If an egg custard sauce begins to curdle or separate, strain it into a clean bowl, add one or two ice cubes and whisk briskly —the temperature of the sauce will be reduced, which should make it smooth once again.

TECHNIQUE TIP: *To prevent a skin from forming on a thickened sauce (such as egg custard), cover the surface of the hot sauce closely with a piece of damp or lightly buttered (butter-side down) parchment paper or plastic wrap.*

CLEVER SOLUTION: When a recipe calls for a sauce or stock to be reduced, an easy way to gauge this is to measure the depth of the sauce in the pan with a clean metal ruler. Work out from the present depth at what level the sauce should be when it has reduced as the recipe directs. Check the depth periodically as the sauce reduces, rinsing the ruler between dippings.

soups

TASTE TIP: *Save the cooking water when boiling or steaming vegetables, and add it to soups, sauces, stocks, or gravies to add extra flavor and nutrients.*

CLEVER SOLUTION: An excellent way of thickening soups is to stir in a little oatmeal. It adds flavor and richness too. A small amount of instant mashed potato stirred in at the last minute is also a good way of thickening soup.

Ground almonds can add body to and enrich soups, as well as boosting flavor and texture. Add a small amount of ground almonds at a time to the blended soup (fish and chicken soups are ideal) and heat gently, stirring, until the soup is thickened to the desired consistency.

TASTE TIP: *A teaspoon or two of pesto sauce stirred into each portion of a hot vegetable soup just before serving will liven it up.*

STORAGE TIP: *For convenient single servings, freeze portions of homemade soup in large, thick paper cups or small individual containers. Remove them from the freezer as required, defrost, and reheat the soup thoroughly before serving.*

Garnish soups so they look attractive and complement the flavor of the soup. You could try chopped fresh herb leaves or whole sprigs of fresh herbs; finely grated cheese such as cheddar or fresh Parmesan; crunchy croûtons (plain or lightly flavored, for example with garlic or ground spices); finely chopped or thinly sliced blanched vegetables such as leeks, carrots, or zucchini; cream, soured cream, or plain yogurt swirled into the soup; finely chopped or crumbled ham or crispy bacon; and finely shredded scallions or watercress.

HEALTHY HINT: Instead of frying croûtons, toss the bread cubes in a little olive oil and seasoning, then spread them on a baking sheet and bake in a preheated moderate oven (about 350°F) for 10–15 minutes, or until they are golden and crisp. For a taste boost, use flavored oil such as chile, herb, or nut oil.

For extra appeal when making croûtons for soup, cut attractive shapes from the bread slices using small biscuit or jelly cutters, rather than cutting them into simple cubes. Toss the fried croûtons in chopped parsley just before serving, if desired.

TASTE TIP: Use specialty bread such as sun-dried tomato or herb bread to make croûtons. Whole-wheat bread also makes good croûtons, and you can add a crushed clove of garlic to the cooking oil for extra flavor.

TASTE TIP: Toss freshly made, warm croûtons in a little finely grated fresh Parmesan cheese, for extra appeal and flavor.

fresh produce

vegetables

STORAGE TIP: *Most vegetables keep best in the refrigerator, but a cool, dark place is also good if you don't have enough fridge space. Potatoes should always be stored in the dark, otherwise they will go green or sprout, making them inedible.*

Starchy or floury potatoes make the best french fries. Their starchiness also makes them the best choice for mashed and roast potatoes.

TECHNIQUE TIP: *Don't use a food processor or electric beaters when mashing potatoes as this is likely to give them an unpleasant gluey texture. Use a potato masher, fork, potato ricer, or food mill. Once the potatoes are mashed you can beat them to lighten the texture, but this is best done by hand with a wooden spoon.*

TECHNIQUE TIP: *To clean leeks effectively, trim them, then slit them lengthwise about a third of the way through. You can then open the leaves a little and wash away any stubborn dirt from between the layers under cold running water.*

CLEVER SOLUTION: If you are preparing small onions for pickling, put them in a heatproof bowl and cover with boiling water. Leave for several minutes, then drain and cool slightly. The skins should peel away more easily.

TECHNIQUE TIP: *An egg slicer is a quick and easy way to slice small mushrooms (one at a time) or small cooked beets into thin, even slices.*

STORAGE TIP: *One leg of an old, clean pair of pantyhose makes a good onion storage unit. Put an onion in the foot end, then tie a knot just above it. Add another onion and tie a further knot above, and so on. This keeps the onions separate and fresh during storage. Keep in a cool, dark place for several weeks.*

TECHNIQUE TIP: *To roast peppers, halve them and place cut-side down on the rack in a broiler pan. Broil for 10–15 minutes, or until the skins have blackened. Remove from the heat, cover with a clean damp kitchen towel or put in a plastic bag, and let cool. Once cool, remove the skin, stalks, cores, and seeds and use as required. Alternatively, push a metal skewer lengthwise through the center of a pepper and hold it (using an oven mitt) over a gas flame, turning regularly, until blackened all over. Cool slightly, then rub off the skin under cold running water.*

CLEVER SOLUTION: An ice cream scoop is an ideal way to remove seeds and strings from vegetables such as squash and pumpkins without damaging the flesh.

TECHNIQUE TIP: *To skin tomatoes, score a small cross in the base of each one using a sharp knife. Put the tomatoes in a heatproof bowl, cover with boiling water, leave for about 30 seconds, then transfer them to a bowl of cold water. When cool enough to handle, drain, and peel off the skins using a paring knife.*

HEALTHY HINT: *Some recipes call for sliced and fried eggplant. Eggplants absorb a lot of oil during frying, so try broiling or baking them instead. Lightly brush the eggplant slices with oil and then broil, or bake them on a nonstick baking sheet in a hot oven, turning once.*

A pastry blender is ideal for chopping whole canned tomatoes in a bowl. Alternatively, a pair of clean kitchen scissors can be used to snip the tomatoes into pieces while they are still in the can.

CLEVER SOLUTION: Use a potato ricer to extract as much water as possible from cooked greens such as spinach. Alternatively, drain in a colander and press out excess moisture with a potato masher.

An easy way to clean mushrooms is to brush over them gently using a clean, soft toothbrush.

CLEVER SOLUTION: When baking stuffed peppers, keep them upright during cooking in the cups of a muffin pan, or cook each one in an ovenproof ramekin dish.

STORAGE TIP: *Keep celery and scallions fresh by standing them upright with the root ends in a pitcher or glass of cold water.*

CLEVER SOLUTION: To minimize tears when preparing an onion, try peeling it under cold running water and leaving the root end intact when chopping.

TASTE TIP: *Add a pinch or two of sugar to cooked tomatoes and homemade tomato sauce to maximize the flavor.*

If boiling sweet potatoes, always cook them with their skins on and peel later, otherwise the white-fleshed sweet potatoes turn gray and the orange-fleshed variety go soggy.

salads

STORAGE TIP: *Keep salad greens fresh by leaving them attached to their stems, if possible, and store in a plastic box or bag in the refrigerator salad drawer.*

CLEVER SOLUTION: To dry salad greens thoroughly before adding dressing, use a salad spinner, then gently toss the leaves in a large bowl with a few sheets of paper towel. The paper should absorb any last drops of water.

Dress salad greens just before serving, or they may wilt. Alternatively, serve the dressing separately.

When making pasta, rice, or potato salads, add the dressing while the pasta, rice, or potato is still warm, so the flavors can be absorbed.

TECHNIQUE TIP: *To make salad dressings or vinaigrettes, put all the ingredients in a clean screw-top jar, seal, and shake well. Alternatively, put the ingredients straight into the salad bowl and whisk together well, before adding the salad.*

For a tasty and creamy salad dressing, mash some blue cheese and stir it into mayonnaise, or a mixture of mayonnaise and plain Greek yogurt.

CLEVER SOLUTION: Soak raw onion rings in cold water for about an hour, then drain and pat dry before using in a salad. This helps prevent the onion flavor overpowering the salad.

TASTE TIP: *Enhance salads by tossing in a handful or two of lightly toasted seeds or chopped nuts just before serving. Good ideas include sunflower, sesame, or pumpkin seeds and hazelnuts, walnuts, pecans, or pistachios. Toasted seeds can also be sprinkled over cooked vegetables.*

fruit

Choose citrus fruits with bright, uniform color that feel heavy for their size. Avoid those with shriveled or bruised skins. Always wash (in warm water) or gently scrub and dry citrus fruits before grating.

TECHNIQUE TIP: *To yield most juice from a citrus fruit, roll it under the palm of your hand on the work surface first. This also makes squeezing easier. Citrus fruit at room temperature also yield more juice.*

If you need the juice and the zest from a citrus fruit, remove the zest first (you can freeze it in an ice-cube tray for future use) before squeezing the juice.

TIME-SAVING TIP: *To chop sticky dried fruit easily, snip it into pieces with clean kitchen scissors or cut with a sharp knife dipped in hot water, lightly brushed with vegetable oil or dusted with flour.*

TECHNIQUE TIP: *Hull fresh strawberries using flat-ended tweezers, to avoid damaging the fruit and to prevent juice-stained fingers.*

To ripen an avocado or fruit such as a hard nectarine or peach, put it in a brown paper bag with a banana and keep at room temperature—ethylene released from the banana will hasten the ripening process.

TECHNIQUE TIP: *To peel peaches or plums, plunge them into a bowl of boiling water for 1 minute, then remove and plunge into cold or iced water to stop the cooking process. When cool enough to handle, the skins will peel off easily.*

A pineapple that has a distinctive, sweet scent will be ripe and ready to eat. Another test for ripeness is to pluck out one of the spiky leaves—if it pulls out easily, the pineapple is ripe.

Rinse fresh berries such as raspberries and strawberries just before serving, as they will deteriorate quickly once washed.

TECHNIQUE TIP: *To keep soft fruits such as raspberries or strawberries separate while frozen, open-freeze them on baking sheets until firm before packing into freezer bags or containers.*

Pit cherries inside a plastic bag to prevent the juice from splattering everywhere.

CLEVER SOLUTION: Use a fork to remove red-, black-, and white currants from their stalks without bruising them. Hold a few small sprigs at a time and gently comb through the stems with the fork, pushing the currants off as you go.

To prevent apples from splitting when baking, either cut a slit around the center or remove a strip of skin from around the stalk.

When making apple sauce, coarsely grate the apples rather than slicing or chopping them—they will cook more quickly and the sauce will be smoother.

Apples and pears are less likely to break up during cooking if they are cooked in a covered dish in a moderate oven, rather than on the stovetop.

TECHNIQUE TIP: *Use a melon baller or a metal measuring teaspoon to remove the core and seeds from halved apples or pears.*

nuts & seeds

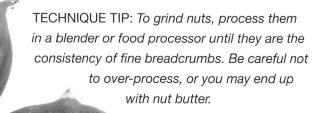

STORAGE TIP: *Nuts have a high fat content so can turn rancid more easily if stored somewhere warm or damp. Buy nuts in small quantities, store in an airtight container in a cool, dry cupboard, and once opened, use them fairly quickly. Some nuts, such as shelled walnuts and blanched almonds, also freeze well.*

TECHNIQUE TIP: *To blanch almonds, put them in a heatproof bowl, cover with boiling water, and leave for 2–3 minutes, then drain and let cool. Rub the nuts in paper towels to remove the skins, or pinch each almond at one end and it should slip out of its skin.*

TECHNIQUE TIP: *To skin whole hazelnuts in a microwave, put them in a shallow dish and microwave on HIGH for 3–4 minutes or until lightly toasted, stirring every 30 seconds. Let cool completely, then rub in damp paper towels or a damp kitchen towel to remove the loosened skins.*

To toast flaked almonds, put them in a small frying pan over moderate heat for 3–5 minutes or until the almonds begin to brown, stirring frequently.

TECHNIQUE TIP: *To grind nuts, process them in a blender or food processor until they are the consistency of fine breadcrumbs. Be careful not to over-process, or you may end up with nut butter.*

SAFETY TIP: *Before roasting or toasting whole chestnuts, make a cross in the skins with a sharp knife to keep the nuts from bursting during cooking.*

TASTE TIP: *Toasting seeds releases their natural oils and brings out their flavor. Ideal varieties include sesame, poppy, cumin, coriander, and mustard seeds. Sprinkle a thin layer of seeds over the bottom of a heavy-based dry skillet. Shake or stir the seeds over low to moderate heat until they are golden or release their fragrance.*

TASTE TIP: *Scatter sweet or savory muffins with a few sunflower seeds before baking, to add extra flavor and crunch.*

Brush homemade or part-baked bread rolls with milk, beaten egg, or salted water, then sprinkle over some sesame, poppy, or caraway seeds before baking, for extra texture and taste.

CLEVER SOLUTION: A metal pastry blender is ideal for chopping softer nuts such as walnuts or pecans in a mixing bowl. It saves the nuts from flying all over the place, which often happens when you chop them on a board.

CLEVER SOLUTION: If marzipan or almond paste has become hard during storage, seal it in a plastic bag with a slice of fresh bread. The moisture from the bread should restore the marzipan to its pliable state.

dairy foods & eggs

butter

STORAGE TIP: *Freeze freshly bought unopened blocks of butter in sealed freezer bags, or wrap them in foil. Salted butter freezes well for up to 3 months and unsalted butter for up to 6 months.*

TECHNIQUE TIP: *When a recipe instructs you to dot butter over the surface, use a coarse grater to grate chilled butter straight from the packet over the dish, or shave chilled butter over the dish using a vegetable peeler.*

TECHNIQUE TIP: *Instead of rubbing butter into flour using your fingertips, try coarsely grating chilled butter into the flour, then using a pastry blender or fork to work it in. This keeps the mixture as cool as possible. A food processor will also do the job quickly and easily.*

TIME-SAVING TIP: *If you need to soften chilled butter quickly, chop it into small pieces and leave in a bowl at room temperature until it is soft enough to use. To soften butter in a microwave, put the (unwrapped) butter in a dish and heat on DEFROST (30% power) for 30 seconds for each stick of butter, or until soft.*

TECHNIQUE TIP: *A melon baller is ideal for making butter balls. Dip the melon baller in warm water first. Gently push each ball of butter out into a bowl of iced water (this will keep the butter balls firm). Store the butter balls in the iced water in the refrigerator until you need them. Drain before use or serve from the bowl.*

When shallow-frying with butter, add a little oil to stop it from burning—butter browns easily and burns at a lower temperature than most vegetable oils. The mixture of butter and oil will give food a rich, golden color.

STORAGE TIP: *Wrap butter well or store it in a covered container in the fridge, as butter picks up strong flavors from foods stored nearby.*

When baking, use the foil wrappers from blocks of butter or hard margarine to grease cake and loaf pans.

CLEVER SOLUTION: If you are creaming butter for a cake mixture and it is slightly too cool, wrap a warm, damp kitchen towel around the bowl and continue to cream.

To make herb or flavored butters, beat unsalted butter until softened, then beat in flavorings such as chopped fresh herbs or crushed garlic with a little lemon juice and seasoning until well mixed. Turn onto a sheet of plastic wrap, shape into a log and wrap in the plastic wrap, then chill in the refrigerator for at least 1 hour before cutting into slices to serve. As a guide, to make herb butter for 4–6, combine 1 stick softened butter with 3–4 tablespoons chopped fresh herbs, 2 teaspoons fresh lemon juice, and salt and black pepper. Herb or flavored butters will keep in the fridge for 2 days or in the freezer for up to 1 month.

cheese

STORAGE TIP: *Store cheese in the fridge in a covered plastic container or loosely wrapped in waxed paper or foil. Do not wrap cheese tightly, as this prevents it from breathing. Do not use plastic wrap, which can make cheese sweat, or butcher paper, which may draw the fat out and encourage mold. Many hard or semi-hard cheeses taste better served at room temperature— remove the cheese from the fridge 1–2 hours before serving to enjoy at its best.*

STORAGE TIP: *Grated hard cheese such as cheddar freezes well, but soft cheese such as Brie and most blue cheese (Stilton is an exception) does not. Grated cheese can be used straight from the freezer.*

TECHNIQUE TIP: *Use a hand-held fine grater when you need a small amount of a hard cheese such as fresh Parmesan. Grate the cheese directly over a dish just before serving.*

TECHNIQUE TIP: *Use a vegetable or potato peeler to shave fresh Parmesan or other hard cheeses. Use a little pressure to make thin shavings and more pressure for thicker shavings.*

TECHNIQUE TIP: *Use an egg slicer to cut fresh mozzarella into neat slices. Cut a standard mozzarella ball in half crosswise, then place one half in the egg slicer. Close the egg slicer to cut through the cheese, then remove the cheese and separate it into individual slices. Repeat with the other half.*

TECHNIQUE TIP: *It's easiest to grate cheese when it is cold. Softer cheeses such as mozzarella grate most easily if you use a coarse grater with large holes. Alternatively, finely chop softer cheese rather than grating it.*

HEALTHY HINT: *When using hard cheese such as cheddar, choose an aged variety and grate it finely, if possible. You won't need to use as much cheese to achieve the desired taste, so saving on calories and fat.*

HEALTHY HINT: *When making a cheese sauce with reduced-fat hard cheese, remove the pan from the heat before adding the cheese to the cooked sauce to save it from overheating. Do this just before serving.*

STORAGE TIP: *Hard cheeses such as cheddar, Gruyère, and Parmesan will keep for up to 3 weeks if stored correctly. Once opened, fresh, soft cheeses should be consumed within 3 days.*

CLEVER SOLUTION: To keep grated cheese in one place, hold the grater and cheese inside a large plastic food bag while grating.

HEALTHY HINT: *Combine grated reduced-fat hard cheese with fresh breadcrumbs, then sprinkle over the top of a baked dish and grill to create a crispy topping. Reduced-fat hard cheese will melt under the broiler, but it will not bubble and brown as its full-fat equivalents do.*

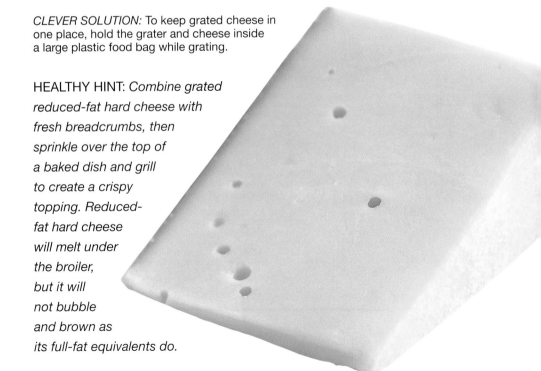

milk & cream

STORAGE TIP: *Homogenized milk can be frozen. Whole milk that is not homogenized tends to separate on thawing, so if you do freeze it, shake it well before use once it has defrosted. Milk can be frozen for up to 1 month, and should be defrosted slowly in the refrigerator. Check the packaging for recommendations for storage and freezing.*

STORAGE TIP: *Freeze milk in waxed cartons or plastic containers with enough room for expansion. Do not freeze milk in sealed plastic bottles without pouring off some of the milk, or the container may split as the milk expands during freezing. Never use glass bottles, which will crack.*

CLEVER SOLUTION: To help prevent milk from scorching during cooking, heat it gently in a heavy-based saucepan or double-boiler. Rinsing the pan in cold water before adding the milk may also keep it from boiling over.

STORAGE TIP: *Cream can be frozen only if it has a butterfat content of 35% or more, so heavy, whipping, and clotted cream are suitable for freezing but light cream is not. Light cream can be frozen if it is incorporated into a dish first. For best results, partially whip the cream to the "floppy" stage before freezing it in plastic containers for up to 2 months. Defrost in the refrigerator overnight or for a few hours at cool room temperature. Open-freeze piped rosettes of whipped cream before putting them in a sealed freezer bag. Arrange the frozen rosettes on your cake or dessert first, then let them defrost for 30–60 minutes at room temperature or 1–2 hours in the fridge.*

TECHNIQUE TIP: *To make cream into soured cream, stir 1–2 teaspoons of freshly squeezed lemon juice into ⅔ cup light or heavy cream. Let stand and the cream will thicken within 15–30 minutes. The heavy cream will thicken more than the light cream.*

To achieve maximum volume of whipped cream, add sugar or other flavorings (such as alcohol or vanilla extract) to lightly whipped cream (when tracks begin to show on the surface), then continue whisking until the cream forms soft or stiff peaks.

TECHNIQUE TIP: *When whipping cream, chill the bowl and whisk beforehand, to keep the cream as cold as possible. Make sure the cream is well chilled too. Use a balloon or spiral whisk rather than electric beaters —the cream will take a little longer to whip but there is less chance of over- whipping (for which there is no remedy).*

CLEVER SOLUTION: To prevent curdling when adding plain yogurt (including Greek yogurt) to hot dishes, remove the cooked dish from the heat and stir in the yogurt just before serving. Do not bring the mixture to the boil again once the yogurt has been added, or the yogurt will curdle.

eggs

STORAGE TIP: *Store eggs in their box in the refrigerator. Keep them pointed-end downwards and away from strong-smelling foods, as they can absorb odors through their shells. Use by the "best-before" date.*

SAFETY TIP: *Wash hands before and after handling eggs, and discard any cracked and/or dirty eggs.*

For many recipes, including cakes and pastry, eggs should be at room temperature. Take them out of the fridge 30–60 minutes before using. Cold eggs may crack when you boil them, and egg whites at room temperature will whisk better than cold egg whites.

STORAGE TIP: *Freeze egg yolks, first mixing them with a little salt or sugar (½–1 teaspoon per two yolks), in a covered plastic container for up to 3 months. Freeze egg whites in a covered plastic container for up to 6 months. Remember to include the number of yolks or whites, and whether they are sweet or salted, on the label. Once thawed, use on the same day and do not refreeze.*

When whisking egg whites, always start with clean, dry, grease-free equipment. Grease, oil, or water in bowls or on whisks will prevent the whites from whisking stiffly. Plastic bowls are not recommended as the surface is difficult to clean completely of oil or grease; use a stainless-steel, glass, china, or ideally copper bowl. Make sure the whites contain no traces of shell or yolks, which contain fat. If a little yolk has fallen into your egg whites, scoop it out, or touch the yolk with a piece of damp kitchen paper— the yolk should stick to the paper. For best results, use very fresh eggs and add a pinch of salt or cream of tartar at the start to help stiffen them.

Make an omelette light and fluffy by folding whisked egg whites into lightly beaten egg yolks before cooking in the usual way.

If you like fried eggs to look neat on the plate, break each one into a greased, round metal cookie cutter (2–3 inches in diameter) in the skillet. Alternatively, use a cookie cutter to trim the whites of fried eggs neatly.

RESCUE REMEDY: If your baked savory soufflé falls, just spoon or slice individual helpings onto plates and serve with a green or mixed salad. Serve a fallen sweet soufflé in spoonfuls, with whipped cream, ice cream, a mixed berry compote, or fruit salad.

Rescue Remedy: If you overcook meringues, cool them, then crush and stir them into ice cream and mixed berries to make a quick dessert. Crushed meringues can also be used in place of chopped nuts to decorate the top and/or sides of cream-covered cakes and gâteaux.

***Rescue Remedy:* If you overcook an omelette, let it cool and use it as a sandwich filling. Chop the omelette and combine it with mayonnaise and snipped fresh chives, if desired.**

meat & poultry

meat

STORAGE TIP: *Fresh meat can be stored in the refrigerator for 2–3 days. Do not exceed the "use-by" date. If you buy meat from a butcher, loosely wrap it in butcher paper or foil before refrigerating.*

TASTE TIP: *Add flavor to fresh sausage meat by kneading in some chopped fresh or dried herbs, or a little dried stuffing mix, before cooking.*

TECHNIQUE TIP: *Cook sausages at a moderate temperature, as they may burst under high heat. Don't prick them before cooking, as this will allow the juices to escape.*

TECHNIQUE TIP: *Putting meat in the freezer for 30–60 minutes before slicing makes it easier to cut thin, even slices as required for recipes such as stroganoff.*

TECHNIQUE TIP: *Produce even-sized meatballs quickly by forming the mixture into a long log, then cutting off even slices and rolling into balls with wet hands.*

Season meat just before grilling, or afterwards, otherwise the salt will draw out the juices and the meat will become dry.

When making a shepherd's pie, beat an egg into the potato topping before covering the pie. Once baked, the pie topping should be tastier and browner.

Once a roast is done, remove it from the oven and let rest on a board in a warm place for 15–30 minutes (depending on size) before carving. This allows the muscles to relax and retain the juices within the meat, keeping it tender and making carving easier. Cover the resting meat loosely with foil to help retain the juices and heat.

TECHNIQUE TIP: *When carving meat, cutting across the grain will give a more regular, tender slice, although it may be easier to carve the underside of some roasts, such as a leg of lamb, more thickly with the grain. Boned roasts are easy to carve, whereas meat on the bone should be carved in stages. Cold cooked joints of meat are much easier to carve than hot, and can be sliced very thinly.*

TECHNIQUE TIP: *When grilling, turn chops, cutlets, and so on with tongs or spoons, to avoid piercing the flesh and losing their juices.*

TASTE TIP: *Add a square or two of dark or bitter chocolate to spicy meat dishes such as chilli con carne, to enhance the flavor and add richness.*

CLEVER SOLUTION: *If you don't have a roasting rack to fit your roasting pan, sit the roast or bird on three or four tight rolls of foil, spaced slightly apart, in the pan instead. Discard the foil after use. Alternatively, celery ribs or thick slices of onion make an edible roasting rack and will flavor the gravy.*

CLEVER SOLUTION: *If a cooked meat stew or casserole looks a little bland, stir in 2–3 teaspoons tomato paste to add body and color.*

Tossing pieces of meat in flour before sealing them helps to lock in the meat juices, as well as adding color to the dish. Flour also helps to thicken the gravy.

poultry

STORAGE TIP: *Fresh poultry will keep for up to 2 days in the refrigerator. Ideally, frozen poultry should be defrosted in the refrigerator and not at room temperature, to minimize bacterial contamination.*

TECHNIQUE TIP: *Raw chicken can be slippery to handle. Use paper towels to hold chicken as you prepare it, or to remove chicken skin.*

Use clean kitchen scissors to cut away any excess fat or tendons from chicken breasts or legs.

TECHNIQUE TIP: *When roasting a whole chicken (or piece of meat), put the bird or meat on a roasting rack in a shallow roasting pan to allow the heat to circulate around the meat and penetrate it more evenly.*

TASTE TIP: *To add flavor to a whole chicken, carefully lift the breast skin and push lemon or orange slices or small fresh herb sprigs underneath before roasting. Herb- or spice-flavored butters can also be spread under the skin before roasting.*

TECHNIQUE TIP: *For crispy duck skin, make sure the skin is as dry as possible before roasting. Prick the dried skin all over with a fork or skewer (but be careful not to pierce the flesh), then rub or sprinkle the bird all over with fine salt and cook it on a rack or trivet in a roasting pan (to allow the fat to drain away).*

Place a whole lemon or peeled onion inside the cavity of a chicken or turkey before roasting, to keep the bird moist and to impart subtle flavor to the meat juices used for gravy.

When pan-frying chicken pieces, leave the skin on to give extra flavor and prevent the chicken from drying out. Remove the skin before serving, if desired.

CLEVER SOLUTION: To flour pieces of chicken or meat, put the flour in a plastic bag, add seasoning, then add the chicken, a few pieces at a time, and shake until thoroughly coated. Shake off any excess coating before cooking.

TASTE TIP: *Brush the skin of a whole chicken with oil, then sprinkle with ground spices (such as curry powder, cumin, or coriander) or chopped fresh or dried mixed herbs before roasting to add flavor, color, and crispness to the skin.*

When buying poultry, choose a bird that looks plump rather than bony, with a creamy white or yellow skin (depending on the variety), without any sign of bruising, blemishes, or dry patches. Larger birds will be more meaty and tend to have a more developed flavor.

CLEVER SOLUTION: To prevent chicken, meat, or vegetables from spinning around on kebab skewers during grilling, thread the pieces onto two skewers held side by side, slightly apart. This method also applies to shelled raw scallops.

cuts of meat & recommended cooking methods

beef

Brisket

Cut from the breast section, brisket is usually sold boneless and is divided in two sections. The flat cut is leaner than the more flavorful point cut. Brisket is best braised. Corned beef is made from brisket.

Chuck

Sold as roasts, steaks, cubed stewing meat, or ground. Best for pot roasts, New England boiled dinner, braises, and stews.

Cube steak

Also called minute steak. A flavorful cut from the top or bottom round that has been tenderized by the butcher by running it through a tenderizing machine. Good for pan-frying.

Flank

The long, thin flank steak is most often marinated and broiled or grilled whole. Thinly slice against the grain before serving.

Ground beef

Also called hamburger. Generally, the lower the price, the higher the fat content. Regular ground beef is usually made from trimmings of the brisket, shank, and other less expensive cuts. The flavorful ground chuck is moderately priced. Leaner ground round and leanest ground sirloin are the most expensive. Suitable for burgers, stuffings, and meat sauces.

Rib

Steaks and roasts are cut from the tender rib section, including the rib eye or Delmonico steak and the standing rib roast.

Round

A large section of beef that extends from the rump to the ankle. Cut into steaks, roasts, strips for stir-frying, and ground. The round is generally tougher than the sirloin and other cuts because this section of the animal gets the most exercise. Suitable for roasting, braising, and pot-roasting.

Short loin

Very tender section of beef cut into tenderloin, T-bone, Porterhouse, and New York strip steaks.

Sirloin

More tender than the round, less tender than the short loin, the sirloin is usually cut into steaks and roasts. Suitable for stir-frying, broiling, grilling, pan-frying, and roasting.

Tenderloin

Also called filet mignon or beef fillet. Very lean and tender cut. Several steaks, including Chateaubriand and Tournedos, are cut from the tenderloin. Suitable for broiling, pan-searing, grilling, stir-frying, and roasting.

lamb

Fillet of lamb

Very lean cut from the loin. Suitable for roasting. Found at specialty butchers.

Ground lamb

Ideal for burgers, meatballs, moussaka, and shepherd's pie.

Leg

Usually sold as a whole leg or half leg roast. Boned and rolled roasts are also available. Suitable primarily for roasting, but can also be braised or grilled over indirect heat. The leg can also be sliced into steaks for pan-frying or grilling, thin strips for stir-frying, or cubes for kebabs or stew.

Loin chops

Sold as loin chops (with traditional small T-shaped bone). Double loin chops may also be available. Suitable for grilling, broiling, pan-searing, frying, or roasting.

Rack of lamb

A portion of the rib section, usually containing eight ribs. The rack can be cut into chops or tied into a crown roast and roasted whole.

Rib chops

Small, tender chops that include a piece of the rib. "Frenched" chops have had tendons cut away from the rib to expose the bone.

Shanks

Suitable for long, slow cooking such as slow-roasting, pot-roasting, and braising.

Shoulder

Sometimes seen as a bone-in or boneless roast when available. Often difficult to find—ask your butcher to save one for you. Suitable for stuffing and roasting, braising, or pot-roasting. More often, cut into cubes and sold for kebabs or stewing.

pork

Boston shoulder (also known as pork shoulder)

Meat from this section is relatively fatty, which makes for tasty, tender, and juicy cuts of pork. Cut into blade roasts and steaks. Suitable for grilling, smoking, broiling, pan-searing, frying, stir-frying, roasting, braising, and stewing. Also, the rectangular Boston butt roast is the cut of choice for pulled pork barbecue.

Ground pork

Perfect for meatballs, meatloaf, burgers, and stuffings for vegetables.

Leg

The hog's hind leg is usually cut into 2 pieces, the shank end and the more tender fillet end. Roasts are called "fresh ham." Steaks are also available. Suitable for roasting, pot-roasting, braising, and stewing. Cured hams are either smoked or salted.

Loin

Pork chops are cut from the loin and include blade chops, loin chops, and rib chops. Bone-in or boneless loin roasts are also popular. Chops can be pan-fried, broiled, grilled, smoked, and roasted. Roasts can be braised, pot-roasted, roasted, or stuffed and roasted.

Picnic shoulder

Actually the foreleg, sold fresh as roasts, steaks, or ground pork. Suitable for roasting, grilling, and braising. Often smoked like ham.

Ribs including spareribs, back ribs and country-style ribs

Spareribs are cut from the belly; back ribs and country-style ribs from the loin. Suitable for slow-roasting, grilling, or smoking.

Tenderloin

Very tender, boneless cut of lean meat sold as a whole fillet. May also be sold as medallions, slices, or escalopes. Suitable for stir-frying, sautéing, pan-searing, grilling, broiling, roasting, or braising.

seafood

fish

When buying whole fresh fish, look for bright, clear eyes, shiny skin and scales, and red or bright pink gills. The flesh should be firm and the outer skin and scales should have a natural slime or film (they should not look dry). Fresh fish should smell fresh and clean. Saltwater fish should smell slightly of the sea, and should not smell strongly fishy or of ammonia. Fish with scales should have an even covering of scales with no large patches of loose scales. Your fishmonger should be happy to gut and scale fresh fish for you, if required.

When buying fresh fish steaks or fillets, choose portions that are firm, plump, and moist, with a fresh, shiny, translucent flesh. Frozen fish should be bought tightly wrapped.

Check with your supplier that the fish you buy has not been previously frozen. If it has, do not refreeze it. Frozen fish is best defrosted slowly in the refrigerator overnight before cooking.

STORAGE TIP: *All fish is very perishable (especially once cut or prepared) and should be stored loosely wrapped or in a covered container in the coldest part of the refrigerator. Fish should be cooked and eaten within 24 hours of purchase.*

CLEVER SOLUTION: Pluck out stray bones from fish fillets using a pair of tweezers.

Choose smoked fish that is plump and shiny, and avoid any that looks shriveled and dry. Avoid artificially colored or dyed fish if possible.

TECHNIQUE TIP: *To scale a fish, grasp it firmly by the tail. Use a fish scaler, vegetable peeler, small sharp knife, or the back of a heavy knife and make short, firm strokes from tail to head to remove the scales, then rinse the fish.*

CLEVER SOLUTION: To remove fishy odors after preparing fish, rub the cut surface of a lemon over your hands, the knife, and chopping board. Rubbing your hands with vinegar or salt, then rinsing and washing them, will also help to get rid of the fishy smell.

When fish is cooked, the flesh becomes opaque and firmer. It should flake with a fork and come away from the bones easily.

TASTE TIP: *Before cooking whole (gutted) fish, tuck fresh herb sprigs or citrus fruit slices into the cavity, so that the flavor penetrates the flesh.*

CLEVER SOLUTION: Brush whole fish and fish fillets with oil before grilling or broiling, to help prevent them from sticking to the grill rack or broiler pan. (This is also a good tip for meats.)

TECHNIQUE TIP: *Raw fish can be slippery to handle, especially when removing the skin from fillets. Use a folded paper towel to hold the tail end of the fish, skin side down, as you cut the flesh away from the skin using a sharp knife, working away from you. Alternatively, dip your fingertips in salt to help you grip.*

TECHNIQUE TIP: *When grilling fish, turn it over using one or two lightly greased narrow spatulas. Try not to pierce the flesh as you will lose valuable juices.*

TECHNIQUE TIP: *To speed up the cooking process when grilling or baking whole fish, use a sharp knife to diagonally slash the skin and flesh of the gutted fish at intervals on both sides before cooking. As the fish is cooking you will be able to see into the flesh to check if it is done. The slashes also encourage even cooking and add an attractive finish to the cooked fish. Brush the fish with a little melted butter or oil during cooking if the flesh begins to dry out.*

When baking fish steaks and fillets, brush them with oil or melted butter to keep them moist. Alternatively, add a topping such as a breadcrumb mixture, chopped fresh herbs, lemon slices, or a sauce.

Microwave ovens are ideal for cooking fish, as the fish retains all its delicate texture, shape, and natural juices. Small and medium whole fish and fish fillets or steaks can all be cooked successfully in a microwave. Before microwaving whole fish, slash the skin in two or three places on both sides so that it does not burst during cooking.

To remove some of the saltiness from canned anchovies, soak them in milk or cold water for 10 minutes, then drain and pat dry before serving.

TECHNIQUE TIP: *To finely chop or mince canned anchovies, press them through a garlic press to create a fine purée.*

STORAGE TIP: *Store smoked salmon in its original packaging in the fridge. Open it 30–60 minutes before serving. Wrap any leftovers, store in the fridge, and use within 2 days. Smoked salmon also freezes well for 2–3 months.*

TASTE TIP: *The longer salmon is smoked for, the stronger the final flavor will be. Most smoked salmon is oak-smoked, but heather-smoked salmon is more aromatic, and peat-smoked may be sweeter and richer. Check the packaging to see what to expect.*

Salmon caviar (sometimes called keta caviar or ikura) is more affordable (and sustainable) than other caviars, but looks and tastes just as good. It is available alongside smoked fish in the chilled sections of some supermarkets, and is often used in sushi.

CLEVER SOLUTION: When removing a cooked large whole fish from the grill or broiler, slide two lightly oiled metal spatulas side by side under the fish to give it support. This will help prevent the fish from breaking or falling apart. Gently lift the fish and transfer it to a serving platter.

shellfish

STORAGE TIP: *Once shellfish die, their flesh deteriorates quickly. Whether live or cooked, shellfish should be kept refrigerated and used within 24 hours of purchase.*

TECHNIQUE TIP: *To devein large shrimp, cut along the back of each shell using kitchen scissors or a small sharp knife, and lift or scrape out the dark vein. Alternatively, use a skewer to pierce the flesh at the head end of the shrimp, just below the vein, then use the skewer to gently remove the vein.*

CLEVER SOLUTION: When grilling or broiling shrimp in their shells, slit the back of each shell with fine scissors. When the shrimp are cooked they will be easier to peel.

When buying live mussels, allow 8–16 ounces of mussels in their shells per person, depending on whether you are serving them as a starter or as an entree.

To prepare fresh mussels, fill a sink with cold water and add the mussels in their shells. Scrape off any barnacles using the back of a small knife, then pull away and discard the beards. Scrub the shells with a stiff brush or scourer, if necessary, to remove any dirt. Discard any mussels with broken shells, or open mussels that don't close when tapped sharply on the work surface. Rinse and drain well. During cooking the mussels will open. Once cooked, discard any mussels that have not fully opened.

Choose fresh oysters with shells tightly shut. Fresh oysters will keep for up to 2 days in the refrigerator. Oysters that have been opened (shucked) are best eaten as soon as possible, but can keep for up to 2 hours in the refrigerator.

When buying a live lobster, choose one that is energetic and heavy for its size. Cooked fresh lobsters are easier to find—look for a firm, springy tail.

Crabs are bought alive or already cooked, in which case they may also be prepared, or dressed. When buying a live crab, choose an active creature. When buying cooked fresh crab, one that feels heavy for its size will contain more meat.

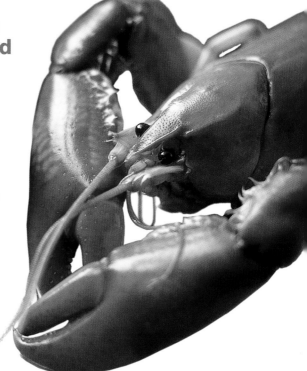

Scallops may have been soaked in saline to make them appear bigger, but once cooked they will shrink to their original size. Look for scallops labeled "dry."

Scallops require brief cooking, usually 2–6 minutes, if grilled, poached, or sautéed, depending on their size and the intensity of the heat used. Do not overcook scallops or they will become rubbery.

To add flavor and to keep them moist, wrap scallops in strips of bacon (cut in half), then thread onto skewers and broil until the bacon is browned and the scallops are cooked and firm to the touch.

beans, grains, pasta, noodles, & rice

beans & grains

STORAGE TIP: *Store dried beans and pulses in airtight containers in a cool, dry, dark place. Make a note of the "best-before" date, and don't mix old and new beans. Older dried beans will take longer to cook than fresh ones.*

Pick over and rinse dried beans before use to remove any grit and debris. Spread dark beans over a white plate or chopping board to make it easier to spot any unwanted bits.

With the exception of dried lentils and split peas, dried beans must be soaked before cooking. This helps the beans cook evenly and more quickly and makes them more digestible. If any dried beans float to the top of the bowl of soaking water, discard them as they may be damaged or moldy. Check the package instructions for soaking and cooking times.

After soaking, raw red kidney beans and soy beans should be fast-boiled for 10–15 minutes to remove harmful toxins they contain. Once fast-boiled, simmer the beans in fresh water until tender.

When cooking beans, never add seasoning until they are done. Salt toughens the skins and prevents the beans from cooking properly and softening. Acidic ingredients such as lemon juice, tomatoes, or wine, added to beans before they are completely cooked, will also toughen the skins.

STORAGE TIP: *Cook more beans than you need, then store the leftover cooled beans in an airtight container in the fridge for up to 2 days or in the freezer for up to 2 months.*

Bulk out a pasta or rice salad by adding a can of drained and rinsed beans such as chickpeas, red kidney beans, black beans, or black-eyed peas. Alternatively, add some canned or frozen corn kernels or cooked (cooled) frozen baby butter beans or peas.

When you are getting to the end of packets of breakfast cereal such as cornflakes or bran flakes, crush the bits left using a rolling pin, then store them in an airtight jar and use as an alternative to breadcrumbs, for example for coating chicken or fish portions.

TASTE TIP: *For added flavor, use good-quality stock (vegetable and chicken are ideal) instead of water to cook couscous or roasted buckwheat.*

Add a little pearl barley to soups and stews— it will add flavor and texture and have a thickening effect.

Use oats or oatmeal in crumble toppings in place of some of the flour to add flavor and texture, or use them to coat fish or chicken portions instead of breadcrumbs before shallow-frying. Oatmeal or rolled oats (ground in a food processor) can be used instead of some of the wheat flour in recipes such as bread, cookies, cakes, and stuffings, to add flavor and texture.

Cut cold, firm, cooked polenta into different shapes (using a sharp knife or cookie cutters) before shallow-frying or grilling, to add interest.

TASTE TIP: *Add flavor to cooked, hot polenta by stirring in chopped fresh mixed herbs or grated fresh Parmesan cheese.*

Semolina can be substituted for some of the wheat flour in some cake and cookie recipes, to add a crisp, slightly gritty texture.

Use millet grain or seed (rinsed and drained) instead of rice to make a tasty and nutritious pilaf.

When making bread in loaf pans or other shaped pans, grease the pan and sprinkle lightly with rolled oats, fine oatmeal, cracked wheat, wheat bran, or oat bran before adding the bread dough, then bake as normal. The baked loaf will have a lovely nutty-flavored crust.

Sprinkle glazed homemade rolls or loaves of bread with wheat, barley, or rye flakes, cracked wheat, or fine cornmeal before baking, to add delicious texture. You could also try brushing the tops of storebought part-baked rolls or loaves with a little salted water or beaten egg and sprinkling with any of the above before baking.

types of pasta

Small tubes and twists such as fusilli and penne are good for chunky vegetable sauces and some meat- and cream-based sauces.

Larger tubes such as rigatoni are ideal for meat sauces.

Smooth, creamy, butter- or olive oil-based sauces and meat sauces are ideal for long strands such as spaghetti (so the sauce can cling to the pasta).

Lasagne, macaroni, and cannelloni work best when baked in recipes.

Bucatini
Long hollow pasta, like thin drinking straws

Cannelloni
Large hollow tubes or rectangular sheets, which are filled and rolled

Capellini
Very fine spaghetti

Conchiglie
Shell-shaped pasta

Farfalle
Bow-tie-shaped pasta

Fettuccine
Long, thin, flat ribbons, slightly narrower than tagliatelle

Fusilli
Short, spiral-shaped pasta

Fusilli Bucati
Slim spiral twists

Gnocchi
Small dried pasta shaped to resemble little potato gnocchi

Lasagne
Large flat sheets

Lasagnette
Flat strips of pasta with wavy edges

Linguine
Narrow, flat strips of pasta

Lumache
Curled, snail-like shapes

Macaroni
Short, hollow tubes

Orecchiette
Small ear-shaped pasta

Pappardelle
Flat, wide strips of pasta

Pastine/Pastina or **Soup Pasta**
Tiny pasta shapes for soups

Penne
Quill-shaped, short tubes, ridged (rigate) or smooth (lisce)

Pipe Rigate
Curved, short, ridged tubes of pasta

Radiatori
Short ridged pasta shapes that resemble old-fashioned radiators

Ravioli
Stuffed pasta shapes, usually square or round

Rigatoni
Large, short, fat, ridged tubes

Ruote di Carro or **Rotelle**
Cartwheel-shaped pasta

Spaghetti
Long, thin, solid strands

Spaghettini
Thin spaghetti

Tagliarini
Thin tagliatelle

Tagliatelle
Long, flat, ribbonlike strands of pasta

Tortellini
Stuffed squares or rounds of pasta, folded in half, curled round, and pinched together to form rings

Tortelloni
Large tortellini

Vermicelli
Long, very thin, fine strands

pasta & noodles

STORAGE TIP: *Dried pasta has a long shelf life and should be stored in its unopened packet or in an airtight container in a cool, dry place. Fresh pasta is best used immediately. Leftover cooked pasta should be kept in a sealed container in the fridge and used within 2 days. Uncooked fresh pasta freezes well for up to 1 month, and can be cooked from frozen, allowing a little extra cooking time. Ordinary cooked pasta does not freeze well on its own, but it freezes successfully in dishes such as lasagne and stuffed cannelloni.*

For a main meal, allow 3–4 oz of dried pasta per person, or 4–5½ oz of fresh pasta. The same quantities apply to stuffed varieties of pasta such as ravioli.

TECHNIQUE TIP: *Pasta must be cooked in a large volume of salted, boiling water. Always add pasta to fast-boiling water and keep the water at a rolling boil throughout cooking. Once you have added the pasta to the boiling water, give it a stir, then cover the pan to help the water return to boiling as quickly as possible. Remove the lid once the water has started boiling again (to prevent the water boiling over), and stir occasionally. Fresh unfilled pasta takes 1–3 minutes to cook and filled 3–4 minutes to cook. When cooking dried pasta, check the instructions on the packet. When it is ready, cooked pasta should be* al dente *—tender but with a slight resistance.*

Do not rinse cooked pasta after draining unless it is being used in a cold dish, as rinsing will wash away the natural sticky starches that help the sauce cling to the pasta. If you are having hot pasta, drain it and serve immediately with the sauce. If serving pasta cold (such as in a salad), rinse it under cold running water to stop the cooking process and drain it well, then toss with olive oil or salad dressing to keep the pieces separate.

Always serve hot pasta on warmed plates or bowls, as drained pasta loses its heat quickly.

HEALTHY HINT: *For a healthier option and to increase your fiber intake, choose whole-wheat or multigrain pasta instead of white pasta.*

Dried noodles (made from wheat and egg, rice, or mung bean flour) need to be softened before use. This is done either by briefly soaking or blanching the noodles in hot or boiling water, or by cooking them in boiling water for a few minutes. Fresh noodles can usually be cooked without any prior preparation.

Cooked noodles are great for adding bulk, texture, and flavor to warm salads and stir-fries. Noodles can also be added to soups towards the end of the cooking time, to make them more substantial.

rice

STORAGE TIP: *Uncooked rice keeps well—store it in its unopened packet or in an airtight container in a cool, dry cupboard and keep an eye on the "best-before" date.*

STORAGE TIP: *Cooked rice is a potential source of food poisoning. Cool leftovers quickly (ideally within an hour), then store in an airtight container in the refrigerator and use within 24 hours. Always reheat cooked cold rice until piping hot.*

As an accompaniment, allow ⅓–½ cup of uncooked rice per person, and for a rice salad or a dish such as risotto, up to ⅔ cup.

Risotto, jasmine, glutinous, and short-grain rices always stick together when cooked. For separate grains, choose an all-purpose long-grain or basmati rice.

Rice may be rinsed before cooking to remove tiny pieces of grit (if you buy it loose) or excess starch. Most packaged rice is checked and clean, however, so rinsing it is unnecessary and will wash away nutrients. Risotto rice is not washed before use, but basmati rice usually is—rinse it under cold running water until the water runs clear.

TECHNIQUE TIP: *Cook rice in a heavy-based pan with a tight-fitting lid and plenty of room, as rice triples in size when cooked. Use a fork to fluff up and separate the cooked grains just before serving.*

TECHNIQUE TIP: *Stir most types of rice once at the beginning of cooking, then do not stir again until it is cooked. Stirring rice during cooking releases the starch in the grains and makes it more sticky. This is why risotto rice is stirred frequently or continuously, to produce its characteristic sticky, creamy texture.*

TASTE TIP: *When boiling or steaming rice, lightly toast the grains by frying in a little oil or melted butter for 1–2 minutes before adding the water or stock, to enhance its flavor. Add a generous pinch of crushed saffron to the cooking water to impart a subtle flavor and yellow shade, or add chopped fresh or dried herbs for extra flavor and color.*

When making a risotto, always use risotto rice such as arborio or carnaroli, as they can absorb plenty of liquid without becoming mushy. Use a well-flavored stock. Remember that the stock should be boiling when added to the rice.

A couple of tablespoons of light cream stirred into risotto just before serving adds extra smoothness.

For rice pudding, always choose short-grain rice, round, or pearl rice, as this absorbs a large quantity of liquid due to its higher starch content, and becomes sticky and very soft during cooking.

TASTE TIP: *To add flavor to plain rice or semolina pudding, stir in the finely grated zest of 1 unwaxed lemon or 1 small orange before cooking.*

baking

bread

When making bread, make sure the liquid is very warm (115–120°F) but not hot. If it is too hot it will kill the yeast. If it is too cold, it will inhibit the yeast's action.

Never add salt directly to yeast as salt can inhibit its growth or kill it.

TASTE TIP: *Use celery salt or garlic salt instead of table salt when making savory bread dough, to add a subtle flavor to the baked loaf.*

Measure ingredients accurately. Too much flour will result in a dry and crumbly loaf; too much liquid may give a dense, flat loaf. If too much yeast is used, the bread is likely to stale very quickly.

TECHNIQUE TIP: *Don't be tempted to add too much flour to the work surface when kneading, as this may make the dough tough and dry. A light sprinkling of flour should suffice.*

To see if dough has doubled in size after the first rising and is ready for punching down, gently insert a floured finger into the center—it should not spring back. Once the dough has risen for a second or final time, press it gently with a floured finger—it should feel springy and soft and the indentation left by your finger should slowly fill in. This means it is ready for baking.

When slashing the top of a loaf before baking, use a sharp knife lightly sprayed with oil to ensure clean, neat cuts.

Pizza dough can be made and kneaded the day before you want to use it, then kept in the fridge in an oiled plastic bag, or in a covered oiled bowl. The dough will rise slowly overnight, and requires a quick knead before you roll it out. This slow-rising method can be applied to many yeasted bread doughs.

STORAGE TIP: *Most homemade bread is at its best on the day it is made, or within 2 days of baking. Enriched breads (with a high fat or sugar content) should keep for up to 3 days. Many storebought breads, especially sliced loaves, have a longer storage life as they contain preservatives or flour improvers.*

STORAGE TIP: *Store bread in a cool, dark, dry place such as a bread box. The cold temperature of a fridge will draw moisture out of the loaf, making it stale.*

STORAGE TIP: *To keep a fresh loaf crusty, store it in a paper or fabric bag. Wrap bread in foil or in a plastic bag if it has a soft crust.*

Money-Saving Idea: Make leftover bread into breadcrumbs and store in the freezer for up to 3 months.

If you have leftover toast or stale bread, bake it in a moderate oven until hard, then leave to cool and crush it with a rolling pin. Store the dried breadcrumbs in an airtight jar for up to 1 month.

cakes

Always use the correct size and depth of cake pan specified in the recipe. A smaller, bigger, or shallower pan may cause a cake to fail.

If you are dividing cake batter between two pans, it is important to divide the mixture evenly. Weigh the filled pans to check.

Most light cakes should be turned out of their pans a few minutes after removal from the oven. Rich fruit cakes are usually left to cool completely in the pan to allow them to solidify before storing and maturing.

TECHNIQUE TIP: *Toss dried fruit, glacé cherries, and nuts in a little flour or ground almonds before adding them to a cake batter. This should prevent the fruit or nuts from sinking to the bottom of the cake and keep them evenly dispersed during baking. If you wash the fruit, dry it well before using.*

Create a crunchy topping for plain cupcakes by sprinkling them with granulated or coarse sugar before baking.

To add a finishing touch to plain sponge cakes, put a paper doily on top of the cake, then sprinkle with sifted confectioners' sugar or sifted cocoa powder. Carefully lift the doily off to reveal a lacy pattern. Alternatively, use strips of paper laid across the cake at intervals to create stripes or a lattice.

TECHNIQUE TIP: *When tinting an icing, use a skewer or toothpick to control the addition of liquid food coloring. Dip the skewer into the bottle, then use it like a dropper. This also works well when you need to add a small amount of concentrated flavoring to recipes.*

CLEVER SOLUTION: If you do not have a piping bag, use a strong plastic bag. Snip a corner off the bottom of the bag, insert a nozzle, then fill with icing and pipe as normal. Discard the bag after use.

Use the tines of a fork to draw wavy patterns in icing, the back of a spoon to create swirls, or the tip of a blunt knife to form peaks.

STORAGE TIP: *Store cakes in an airtight container, or wrap with foil or plastic wrap, and store in a cool, dry place. Wrap rich fruit cakes in waxed or parchment paper before wrapping in foil, otherwise the fruit may react with the foil. Cream cakes should be kept in a covered container in the fridge.*

TECHNIQUE TIP: *Cut scone dough into squares or triangles rather than rounds, so there won't be any trimmings to roll and you won't need a cookie cutter.*

CLEVER SOLUTION: When making muffins, buns, or cupcakes, lightly spray the paper cases with vegetable oil before use. They should then peel off more easily after baking.

Rescue Remedy: If a cake breaks, stick the pieces together with jam or icing, then ice or cover the cake with another topping.

pastry

Always chill pastry dough for 30 minutes before rolling it (then ideally chill it again for 20–30 minutes before baking). This helps to prevent excessive shrinking during baking, and also keeps the pastry from cracking when it is rolled out.

TECHNIQUE TIP: *Stack trimmings of puff or flaky pastry on top of each other, rather than pressing them into a ball, before rolling them again. This will help to keep the important layers intact.*

TECHNIQUE TIP: *When making quiches or tarts, the edges of the pastry case should be flush with the rim on the pan or dish. When the pastry has been pressed into the pan, run a rolling pin over the top of the pan to break off any excess.*

TECHNIQUE TIP: *To cover a pie with a pastry lid, lift the rolled-out pastry to the pie on a rolling pin and carefully unroll over the filling. Alternatively, fold the pastry into quarters, transfer it to the dish with the point in the center, then unfold.*

CLEVER SOLUTION: Brushing the base of an unbaked pastry shell with egg white or beaten egg will help prevent it becoming soggy. If you're baking a pastry shell blind, remove the beans and brush the base with egg 5 minutes before the end of the cooking time. An alternative is to brush a cold, baked pastry shell with a thin layer of melted chocolate. Let the chocolate set before adding the cold filling.

Toss fruit in a little flour (or flour mixed with ground spices) or cornstarch before filling a pie with it. The flour will help the juices thicken during cooking, which also helps prevent soggy pastry and juices leaking from the pie during baking.

CLEVER SOLUTION: Place a sheet of foil or a large baking sheet on the shelf in the oven below a fruit pie, to catch any drippings.

CLEVER SOLUTION: Cut two slices in a whole pie or cake before removing any portions. This will make it much easier to remove a neat and intact first slice.

When working with phyllo pastry, keep the sheets covered with plastic wrap. Otherwise, the phyllo sheets may dry out and crack, becoming brittle and unusable.

CLEVER SOLUTION: If you don't have a rolling pin, use a straight-sided wine bottle instead. If possible, chill the bottle before rolling to keep the pastry cool as you work.

TECHNIQUE TIP: *To prevent a soggy pastry lid on a pie and to keep it crisp, cut a hole, cross, or several slashes in the top before baking, to allow steam to escape.*

Money-Saving Idea: **Use pastry trimmings to make biscuits. Gently knead in flavorings such as dried coconut and sugar, finely chopped nuts, chopped herbs and grated cheese, or poppy seeds, then cut into small rounds or shapes and bake in a moderate oven until crisp and golden brown.**

cookies

When making cookies, butter tends to result in crisper cookies and margarine tends to make softer cookies.

CLEVER SOLUTION: To keep parchment paper in place on baking sheets when spooning out soft cookie dough, weigh the paper down in each corner with fridge magnets (remove them before baking). Alternatively, lightly spray the baking sheet with oil before lining it with paper.

TECHNIQUE TIP: An easy way to transfer sticky cookie dough to a baking sheet is to use a small ice cream scoop. Dip the scoop into a bowl of cold water between each use to ensure an easy release. This also saves your hands getting messy.

STORAGE TIP: When making a batch of cookies, double the quantity and make some for the freezer too. Place the balls, spoonfuls, or shapes of dough on a baking sheet lined with parchment paper. Open-freeze until firm, then transfer to a freezer bag or plastic container and return to the freezer. Bake from frozen, increasing the original cooking time by a few minutes. Most cookie doughs keep well in a freezer for up to 1 month.

RESCUE REMEDY: If baked cookies are stuck to the baking sheet, return the baking sheet to the oven briefly—the cookies should then lift off easily.

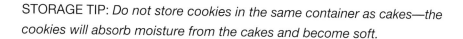

STORAGE TIP:
*Many homemade
cookies freeze
well. Seal them
in freezer bags or
pack in rigid, airtight,
plastic containers and
freeze for up to 3 months. Defrost
for several hours at room temperature.*

STORAGE TIP: *Do not store cookies in the same container as cakes—the cookies will absorb moisture from the cakes and become soft.*

Rescue Remedy: Revive soft cookies that have begun to harden by placing a small slice of fresh bread in the container with them.

STORAGE TIP: *If you place a sugar lump or two in a cookie jar, this will help to keep the cookies crisp and fresh for longer.*

TASTE TIP: *Liven up plain sugar cookies. Once baked and cooled, dip half of each cookie into melted chocolate and let dry on a sheet of waxed paper. You can also top the melted chocolate with decorative sprinkles, finely chopped nuts, or dried coconut before letting set.*

When baking more than one batch of cookies, once you remove each sheet of baked cookies from the oven, let the oven return to the correct cooking temperature before putting in the next batch.

CLEVER SOLUTION: *If you have leftover icing, use it to sandwich together some cookies in pairs. Kids will love them.*

TIME-SAVING TIP: *To cut cookie dough quickly, roll the dough into a long sausage shape, then cut it into even slices using a sharp knife.*

sweet things

desserts

TASTE TIP: *For extra-crunchy crumble topping, replace about 1 oz (¼ cup) of the flour with the same weight of chopped nuts, rolled oats, oatmeal, or crushed amaretti biscuits. Alternatively, sprinkle a loose, uncooked bar mixture over the fruit (do not press it down).*

TIME-SAVING TIP: *Make a double quantity of crumble topping and freeze half for next time. Break into small pieces and sprinkle it over the fruit before baking —there is no need to defrost it first.*

To add a richer flavor to pancakes or crêpes, and to help prevent them sticking to the pan, stir 1–2 tablespoons of melted butter or oil into the batter.

When making dried fruit compotes, use warmed fruit juice or scented tea (such as Earl Grey) for the soaking liquid, and add whole spices such as cinnamon sticks or star anise for extra flavor.

Instead of topping a fruit pie with a solid pastry lid, lay pastry strips over the filling to create a lattice effect, then bake as normal.

To make a crisper, browner lemon meringue pie topping, sprinkle sugar over the meringue just before baking.

TECHNIQUE TIP: *To remove set cold desserts from their molds, briefly dip the mold in hot water before inverting the mold onto a serving plate.*

ice cream & sorbet

Soften hard homemade ice cream in the refrigerator for 20–30 minutes before serving, to make scooping easier. Ice cream should not be allowed to soften too much and then be refrozen, as this will affect its texture and may cause food poisoning.

Save squeezed halved oranges or large lemons, with remaining flesh removed, to use as serving "cups" for ice cream and sorbet. Cut a small slice off the base, if necessary, to stabilize them. If you are not using them immediately, open-freeze them, then store in a sealed bag in the freezer.

CLEVER SOLUTION: Ice crystals can form on the surface of opened tubs of ice cream. To help prevent this, cover the ice cream left in the tub with plastic freezer wrap or waxed paper, pressing it onto the surface before replacing the lid and returning to the freezer.

To make a quick fruit sauce ideal for serving with ice cream and sorbet, purée soft, ripe fruits such as raspberries, strawberries, peeled nectarines, or cooked blackcurrants, then press the purée through a nylon sieve. Gradually whisk in sifted confectioners' sugar to taste and add a dash of fruit liqueur, if desired. Serve warm, cold, or chilled.

Serve iced desserts in chilled dishes to keep them cold when served, especially on hot days. Put the empty dishes in the freezer for a few hours before use.

sugar

STORAGE TIP: *Sometimes brown sugar becomes hard during storage, due to exposure to air. Add a wedge or two of fresh apple or a slice of fresh bread to the sugar container and the moisture should be restored within a couple of days.*

TIME-SAVING TIP: *If you need to use hardened brown sugar immediately, try grating it or blend it in a food processor to break it up.*

TECHNIQUE TIP: *Use a small, heavy-based saucepan to make caramel. This will allow the sugar to caramelize slowly, preventing the mixture from burning and sticking. If the caramel does stick to the pan, carefully add a little cold water and heat gently, stirring, until it has dissolved.*

TASTE TIP: *Pare long, thin strips of lemon, orange, or lime zest, bury the strips in a jar of sugar and leave for a few days before use. The infused sugar can be used to add a delicate flavor to sweet recipes.*

TASTE TIP: *Bury one or two vanilla beans in a jar of granulated sugar and leave for at least a week before use. The sugar will gradually absorb the flavor of the vanilla, and the beans will keep for a long time if stored this way. Use the vanilla sugar to impart a subtle flavor to cakes, cookies, and desserts.*

honey, syrup, & jam

Rescue Remedy: **If honey or syrup hardens during storage, stand the jar in a bowl of hot water for a few minutes or until the honey becomes liquid, rotating the jar occasionally. Alternatively, put the opened jar in a pan of hot water and heat gently, stirring the honey occasionally, until it is runny again. You can also heat the open jar in a microwave on HIGH for 10 seconds at a time, stirring between bursts, until the honey is smooth.**

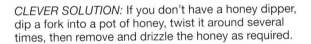

CLEVER SOLUTION: If you don't have a honey dipper, dip a fork into a pot of honey, twist it around several times, then remove and drizzle the honey as required.

CLEVER SOLUTION: When measuring sticky foods such as honey, syrup, or molasses, lightly spray the measuring spoon or jug with oil first. The sticky ingredient should slip out of the spoon or jug easily. Alternatively, use a metal measuring spoon dipped in hot water.

Apricot jam makes an ideal glaze for brushing over rich fruit cakes (such as Christmas cake) before adding marzipan, or for glazing fruit tarts. Put some apricot jam in a pan with a little water or lemon juice. Heat gently, stirring, until the jam has melted and combined with the water. Press through a nylon sieve and use while warm. Cranberry or redcurrant jelly can be combined with a little lemon or orange juice, then warmed until smooth, and used as a glaze for fresh fruit tarts.

chocolate

Rescue Remedy: If you are melting chocolate and it seizes (becomes stiff and grainy), it has been overheated. Take it off the heat and stir in 1–2 teaspoons of vegetable oil, a few drops at a time, until the chocolate is smooth. However, if the chocolate is very scorched it may be unusable. Keep chocolate dry when melting it, as a single drop of water or steam will cause it to seize.

If you add a liquid to melted chocolate, warm it first, as cold liquid may cause the melted chocolate to solidify. Alternatively, add a small amount of liquid to solid chocolate pieces, then melt the chocolate and liquid together. If the chocolate seizes, add a little more liquid and gently heat and stir until it becomes smooth again.

TECHNIQUE TIP: *To grate chocolate without it becoming sticky, use small pieces of well-chilled chocolate, brushing the grater with a dry pastry brush every so often. For best results, use a food processor. Grated chocolate can be frozen.*

TECHNIQUE TIP: *To make chocolate leaves, wash and dry some fresh, shiny rose leaves with a short stem. Brush several layers of melted chocolate onto the veined underside of each leaf and leave to set on a sheet of nonstick baking paper. Once dry, carefully peel each leaf away from the chocolate using its stem. Store in an airtight container in a cool place.*

TECHNIQUE TIP: *To make chocolate decorations, line a baking sheet with waxed or parchment paper. Melt a little chocolate and put it in a paper piping bag or small plastic bag, then cut the tip off the bottom corner. Pipe simple designs onto the paper. Let set, then carefully peel the paper away from the shapes.*

To make fine chocolate curls, spread melted chocolate evenly over a cool surface (such as a marble slab) and leave until just set. Pull a citrus zester across the chocolate. For larger curls, pull the edge of a thin sharp knife at an angle of about 20 degrees through the chocolate. The chocolate should roll into curls or cigarette shapes. Alternatively, make shavings from a large bar of chocolate using a swivel vegetable peeler.

CLEVER SOLUTION: Pick up chocolate shavings with tweezers or a toothpick to position them on a cake or dessert—this way the chocolate won't melt in your fingers.

To shape chocolate truffle mixture into balls, use a melon baller dipped in hot water. Alternatively, coat your hands lightly with vegetable oil and roll the mixture between your palms.

reference

food safety

Keep your kitchen clean and tidy, and disinfect counters after use with a mild detergent or an antibacterial cleaner. As far as possible, keep pets out of the kitchen.

STORAGE TIP: *Store food safely to avoid cross-contamination. Keep food in clean, dry, airtight containers, always store raw and cooked foods separately, and wash utensils (and your hands) between preparing raw and cooked foods. Never put cooked food on a surface that you have used to prepare raw meat, fish, or poultry without thoroughly washing and drying the surface first.*

STORAGE TIP: *Store raw meat and fish on the bottom shelf in the fridge to prevent it dripping onto anything below.*

Never put hot food into a refrigerator, as this will increase the internal temperature to an unsafe level. Cool leftover food quickly to room temperature, ideally by transferring it to a cold dish, then refrigerate. Cool large dishes such as casseroles by putting the dish in a sink of cold or ice water. Stir occasionally (and change the cold water often to keep the temperature low), then refrigerate once cool. During cooling, cover the food loosely to protect it from contamination.

Don't use perishable food beyond the "use-by" date as it could be a health risk. If you have any doubts about the food, discard it.

Do not overfill your fridge; if cold air cannot circulate properly, pockets of warm air may form as a result.

If nonperishable food is eaten after its "best-before" date (within reason), it should not cause any harm but its appearance, flavor, and texture may be past their best.

STORAGE TIP: *Store leftovers in airtight containers or wrap in plastic wrap or foil, and keep in the refrigerator. Always eat leftovers within 2 days.*

Bacteria multiply quickly between 41–149°F, so food should either be kept or served cold or very hot. Ideally, the center of hot food should reach at least 158°F for at least 2 minutes, to ensure that most harmful bacteria are destroyed. The internal temperature of some cooked meats and poultry needs to reach a higher level than this (see page 89), to be sure they are safe to eat. Meat thermometers are useful for checking this.

Reheated food must be piping hot throughout before consumption. Never reheat any type of food more than once.

Raw or lightly cooked eggs (found in homemade mayonnaise, some chilled mousses, soufflés, and other desserts, ice cream, sorbet, and egg drinks) are not recommended for people in higher-risk groups such as babies and young children, pregnant women, the elderly, and those who are ill or convalescing.

Frozen meat and poultry should be thoroughly defrosted before you cook them, otherwise the center may not be cooked when the outside looks done, which could be dangerous.

preserving

TECHNIQUE TIP: *Always use heat-tempered canning jars with two-piece canning lids. The sealing disks can be used only once, but the screw bands can be reused as long as they are in good condition.*

TECHNIQUE TIP: *To sterilize canning jars before filling them, wash in hot, soapy water and then boil in a hot-water bath for 10 minutes. Invert onto a clean towel.*

Use a wide, heavy-bottomed non-reactive stainless steel, aluminum, or enameled cast-iron pan to cook preserves. Traditional copper or brass pans can be used for jams and jellies, but they are not suitable for soaking fruits or making pickles or chutneys containing acidic ingredients like vinegar, as the acid may corrode the metal.

Choose fruit that is just ripe or slightly under-ripe for jams and jellies, as this will contain the most pectin, which is needed to make the jam set properly. Overripe fruit contains much less pectin. Pectin content varies greatly from one type of fruit to another.

CLEVER SOLUTION: *Warm a candy thermometer in hot water before use to prevent it from cracking.*

TIME-SAVING TIP: *When making jam with cherries, plums, or other stone fruits, wash the fruit before use, but don't remove the pits. Once the jam is boiling, the pits will float to the surface and can be skimmed off.*

SAFETY TIP: *Don't fill preserving pans more than half full, to prevent the hot jam from boiling over or splashing too much.*

Once the sugar has dissolved in your jam but before it boils, add a tablespoon of unsalted butter to reduce scum on the surface.

TECHNIQUE TIP: *Long, slow cooking is best for chutneys, so the ingredients can soften and combine to create the maximum flavor and ideal texture.*

STORAGE TIP: *Store chutneys, pickles, and relishes for at least 1 month (preferably 2–3 months) before eating, to allow the flavors to develop.*

CLEVER SOLUTION: Warm the sugar before adding it to the softened fruit, so that it will dissolve quickly and help give a clear set to sweet preserves.

TECHNIQUE TIP: *When making jams or marmalade with pieces of whole fruit, let the jam stand for 15 minutes once cooked. When the mixture has begun to set, stir it to distribute the fruit or peel evenly, then ladle into sterilized jars. This should help prevent the fruit or peel from rising to the top of the jars when fully set.*

CLEVER SOLUTION: If your chosen jelly or jam fruit has a lower pectin content, such as strawberries, peaches, or rhubarb, use jelling sugar (ordinary cane sugar to which natural apple pectin or citric acid is added), or add lemon juice and liquid or powdered pectin. Alternatively, combine a lower-pectin fruit with a high-pectin fruit, such as strawberries with raspberries.

freezing

Freeze food that is in prime condition, on the day of purchase, or as soon as a dish is made and cooled. Freeze food quickly and in small quantities, if possible. Label and date food and keep a good rotation of stock in the freezer.

Always leave a gap in the container when freezing liquids, so that there is enough room for the liquid to expand as it freezes.

Always let food cool before freezing. Warm or hot food will increase the internal temperature of the freezer and may cause other foods to begin to defrost and spoil.

It is important to thaw food slowly, as rapid thawing can lead to moisture loss and dry, tasteless food. Thawing overnight or for several hours in the refrigerator is ideal. Cover food loosely while it is thawing. Do not refreeze food once it has thawed.

CLEVER SOLUTION: When freezing items such as burgers or chops, stack them with a piece of waxed or parchment paper between each one, then put them in freezer bags and freeze for up to 2 months. You can then remove individual portions as needed.

Freeze leftover wine in an ice-cube tray. Once solid, transfer the wine cubes to a freezer bag. The wine cubes can be added to casseroles, stews, and gravies for extra flavor.

SAFETY TIP: *Handle food to be frozen as little as possible and keep everything clean. Freezing does not kill bacteria or germs.*

Rescue Remedy: In a power outage, don't open the freezer door, to prevent warm air entering. Wrap the freezer in a blanket if possible to increase insulation, but do not cover the condenser or pipes at the rear. The food should stay safely frozen for around 26 hours in an upright freezer, or around 30 hours in a chest freezer, provided the door has not been opened and the freezer is reasonably full. If you think that anything has begun to defrost, throw it out.

Freezers use more energy to keep empty spaces cold, so fill gaps with loaves of bread or similar basic foods.

Freezer burn causes dry, grayish white patches on the surface of frozen food when it is exposed to air. Although the food may have lost a little of its moisture, color, and texture, it should be safe to eat.

STORAGE TIP: *If you freeze food in a plastic container, once it has frozen solid, briefly dip the container in hot water to release its contents in a block. Transfer this to a freezer bag, return to the freezer, and the container can be reused.*

Spirits with an alcohol content of 35% or over can be kept in the freezer—this is ideal for those served ice-cold.

entertaining

TIME-SAVING TIP: *Open-freeze slices of lemons, limes, or oranges on a baking sheet lined with parchment paper. Once solid, transfer to a freezer bag. Add the frozen slices to drinks, as required.*

Keep party food bite-sized and simple, so that guests can eat the food easily with one hand, while holding a glass in the other.

When preparing food for a picnic, make individual pies, quiches, or tartlets, as they are more robust than a slice from a larger pie, quiche, or tart, and more practical, making serving and eating easier.

TASTE TIP: *When preparing party nibbles, use pretzel sticks, short lengths of celery rib, or sticks cut from large white radishes to pierce bite-sized items such as cubes of semi-hard cheese, rolls of prosciutto, beef, or smoked salmon, or cocktail sausages. The whole thing can be eaten and it saves having to dispose of toothpicks.*

CLEVER SOLUTION: When steaming vegetables, heat the serving dish by inverting it over the steaming basket or pan (it will act as a lid). Remove the dish using an oven mitt, as it will be hot.

Make ice cubes from different colored fruit juices, then pop into children's party drinks for extra appeal.

CLEVER SOLUTION: If you need to chill a bottle of white or sparkling wine quickly, put it in the freezer for about 30 minutes, and no longer than 45 minutes. Set a timer, otherwise you may forget and end up with an exploded bottle.

CLEVER SOLUTION: Warm up a bottle of red wine by putting it in an ice bucket of warm water (at a temperature of about 68°F) for 20–30 minutes.

TASTE TIP: *Whole star anise will add a rich, spicy flavor to mulled wine.*

At drinks parties, one 750 ml bottle of wine or champagne will give about 6 glasses. Allow at least 2 glasses per person.

CLEVER SOLUTION: If you are short of fridge space, chill bottles of wine, soft drinks, and water in large plastic boxes (coolers are ideal) or buckets packed with ice, then topped up with cold water.

Slice whole fresh strawberries, keeping the slices attached to the green tops, then fan out the slices and use to decorate desserts.

For extra appeal when making sandwiches, use a couple of different loaves. For example, use one slice of whole-wheat and one slice of white bread, or try one slice of rye bread and one slice of 7-grain bread.

Tuck small sprigs of fresh herbs, herb flowers, or garden flowers (tied with ribbon or raffia) into plain napkin rings. Alternatively, tie freshly cut long chives around rolled-up napkins.

Freeze small pieces of fruit in ice cubes and add them to drinks and cocktails, for extra appeal.

microwaving

The more food you are cooking, and the colder it is, the longer it will take to cook in a microwave.

When microwaving items such as sausages or bacon that may spit during cooking, cover them loosely with paper towels, to avoid too much splattering.

SAFETY TIP: *Some whole foods such as eggs, potatoes or apples in their skins, peppers, and sausages should be pricked several times before cooking, otherwise they may burst due to a buildup of steam under the membrane or skin.*

Many foods need to be covered during microwaving. Use microwave-safe plastic wrap, a plate, or a lid. Pierce plastic wrap, or leave a gap at one side if using a plate or lid, to allow excess steam to escape.

SAFETY TIP: *Never operate a microwave oven when it is empty, as the microwaves will bounce back to and damage the oven components.*

SAFETY TIP: *Be careful when stirring heated liquids in a container in the microwave, as they can bubble up without warning.*

After food has been removed from the microwave, it will continue to cook due to the residual heat within the food, so adhere to standing times when they are given in recipes.

TECHNIQUE TIP: *Use a microwave oven with a built-in turntable if possible, and make sure that you turn or stir the food several times during cooking to ensure even cooking throughout. The food toward the outer edges usually cooks first.*

SAFETY TIP: *Take care when removing the cover from a microwave container as the steam inside will be very hot.*

Unless your microwave oven has a broiler element (combination oven), the food will not brown during cooking.

CLEVER SOLUTION: Microwaved foods can look pale and insipid. Enhance the color of sweet dishes by sprinkling them with toasted coconut, brown sugar, cinnamon sugar, or ground spices. Icing will hide a pale cake. To enhance the color of savory dishes, top with toasted chopped nuts or paprika, brush meat or poultry with a little soy sauce or barbecue sauce, or use a basting sauce containing paprika, tomato paste, or mustard.

Metal containers, china with a metallic trim, foil, or crystal glass (which contains lead) should not be used in a microwave. Metal reflects microwaves and may damage the oven components. Microwave-safe plastic containers, ovenproof glass, and ceramic dishes are all suitable, as is most household glazed china. Paper plates and kitchen paper can be used to reheat food for short periods. Roasting bags (pierced) may be used in a microwave.

TIME-SAVING TIP: *Cook vegetables in a heatproof serving dish to save on washing up.*

When cooking cakes in a microwave, make sure you only fill the container half full to allow the cake to rise.

weights & measures

Follow imperial or metric measures, not a mixture of both, as they are not interchangeable. Spoon measures given in recipes are usually for level spoons, unless stated otherwise.

WEIGHT

Metric	Imperial
5 g	⅛ oz
10 g	¼ oz
15 g	½ oz
20 g	¾ oz
25 g	1 oz
40 g	1½ oz
50 g	1¾ oz
55 g	2 oz
70 g	2½ oz
75 g	2¾ oz
100 g	3½ oz
115 g	4 oz
125 g	4½ oz
140 g	5 oz
150 g	5½ oz
175 g	6 oz
200 g	7 oz
225 g	8 oz
250 g	9 oz
300 g	10½ oz
350 g	12 oz
400 g	14 oz
450 g	1 lb
500 g	1 lb 2 oz
600 g	1 lb 5 oz
675 g	1½ lb
700 g	1 lb 9 oz
800 g	1¾ lb
900 g	2 lb
1 kg	2¼ lb
1.5 kg	3 lb 5 oz
2 kg	4½ lb
2.5 kg	5½ lb
3 kg	6½ lb

VOLUME

Metric	Imperial
30 ml	1 fl oz
50 ml	2 fl oz (¼ cup)
75 ml	2½ fl oz (⅓ cup)
100 ml	3½ fl oz
125 ml	4 fl oz (½ cup)
150 ml	5 fl oz (⅔ cup)
175 ml	6 fl oz (¾ cup)
200 ml	7 fl oz or ⅓ pint
225 ml	8 fl oz
250 ml	9 fl oz (1 cup)
275 ml	9½ fl oz
300 ml	10 fl oz or ½ pint
350 ml	12 fl oz
400 ml	14 fl oz
425 ml	15 fl oz or ¾ pint
450 ml	16 fl oz
500 ml	18 fl oz
600 ml	20 fl oz or 1 pint
700 ml	1¼ pints
850 ml	1½ pints
1 litre	1¾ pints
1.2 litres	2 pints
1.3 litres	2¼ pints
1.4 litres	2½ pints
1.5 litres	2¾ pints
1.7 litres	3 pints
2 litres	3½ pints
2.5 litres	4½ pints
3 litres	5¼ pints
4.5 litres	8 pints

SPOONS

Metric	Imperial
1.25 ml	¼ teaspoon
2.5 ml	½ teaspoon
5 ml	1 teaspoon
10 ml	2 teaspoons
15 ml	1 tablespoon or 3 teaspoons
30 ml	2 tablespoons

OTHER USEFUL EQUIVALENTS

1 stick butter = 4 oz = 115 g
1 American pint = 16 fl oz (2 cups) = 450 ml
1 imperial pint = 20 fl oz = 600 ml
1 American cup = 225 ml (8 fl oz)
1 Australian cup = 250 ml (9 fl oz)
1 gallon (UK) = 4.5 litres
1 gallon (US) = 3.8 litres

oven temperatures

Note that all ovens vary. As a guide, if you have a fan-assisted oven, you need to reduce the temperature by 68°F, and/or adjust the cooking times. Refer to the manufacturer's handbook for more information if you have a fan-assisted oven.

Temp.	Centigrade/ Celsius (°C)	Fahrenheit (°F)	Gas
Very Cool	110	225	1/4
	120	250	1/2
Cool	140	275	1
	150	300	2
Warm	170	325	3
Moderate	180	350	4
Fairly Hot	190	375	5
	200	400	6
Hot	220	425	7
	230	450	8
Very Hot	240	475	9

roasting poultry

The internal temperature of cooked poultry should reach 176–185°F.

For CHICKEN, weigh the prepared bird and allow 20 minutes per pound, plus 20 minutes. Roast at 425°F for the first 15 minutes (if desired), then at 375°F for the remaining time or until the juices run clear when the thickest part of the thigh is pierced with a skewer.

For DUCK, weigh the prepared bird and allow 20–25 minutes per pound, slightly longer if you like it well cooked. Roast at 375°F.

For GOOSE, weigh the prepared bird and allow 15 minutes per pound, plus 15 minutes. Roast at 400°F.

roasting turkey

Weigh the turkey after it has been stuffed (you may need to use your bathroom scale). The following guide is for whole turkeys covered loosely with foil and roasted at 375°F. (Remove the foil about 40 minutes before the end of the cooking time to brown the skin, if desired.) If your turkey weighs less than 9 lb, allow 10 minutes per pound, plus 70 minutes. If your bird weighs 9 lb or more, allow 10 minutes per pound, plus 90 minutes.

To test if a turkey is fully cooked, push a skewer into the deepest part of each thigh—if the juices run clear, it is cooked.

roasting meat

The times given below are for guidance only. An instant-read meat thermometer is the most accurate way to test if a joint is cooked sufficiently. Insert into the thickest part of the cooked meat (away from any bones) and leave for 30 seconds to gain an accurate reading. Bone-in roasts cook faster than boneless roasts.

To calculate the roasting time accurately, weigh the meat once it is ready for the oven (after stuffing). Roast in a preheated oven at 425°F for the first 15 minutes, then at 350°F for the remaining time.

Meat	Cooking Time	Internal Temperature
BEEF		
Rare	15–20 minutes per pound, plus 15–20 minutes	140°F
Medium	20–25 minutes per pound, plus 20–25 minutes	160°F
Well Done	25–30 minutes per pound, plus 25–30 minutes	170°F
LAMB		
Medium	20–25 minutes per pound, plus 20–25 minutes	160–167°F
Well Done	25–30 minutes per pound, plus 25–30 minutes	170°F
PORK		
Well Done	30–35 minutes per pound, plus 30–35 minutes	165°F
VEAL		
Well Done	25–30 minutes per pound, plus 25–30 minutes	170°F

glossary

Acidulated water

Water with lemon juice or vinegar added. Used to prevent discoloration in some prepared fruit and vegetables.

Al dente

Italian term describing food that is cooked but still has slight resistance or firmness to the bite.

Au gratin

A savory dish sprinkled with breadcrumbs and/or grated cheese and browned under the broiler. Also, a savory dish covered with cheese sauce or grated cheese and baked in the oven.

Bain-marie

A "water bath" used to cook delicate foods such as egg custards and sauces at a constant temperature. The food is placed in a dish over a pan of simmering water, or in a baking tin half filled with hot water. A double-boiler is also a bain-marie.

Bake blind

To bake an empty pastry shell in a tin before filling. The pastry shell is lined with greaseproof paper, then filled with baking beans to prevent it rising and losing its shape during cooking.

Bard

Thin layers of fat, usually bacon or pork fat, are wrapped or tied around lean cuts of meat, poultry breast meat, or terrines. Barding keeps the meat moist during cooking.

Baste

To spoon cooking juices, melted fat, liquid, or a marinade over food during cooking, to prevent the food drying out and to add flavor.

Beurre manié

Equal quantities of plain flour and softened butter kneaded together to form a paste, which is used for thickening dishes such as soups, sauces, and stews.

Blanch

To immerse food in boiling water briefly, so it is only partly cooked. Once blanched, the food is plunged into cold water to stop the cooking process. Blanching is used to loosen fruit or vegetable skins or to preserve the color, flavor, texture, and nutrients of vegetables prior to freezing.

Brûlé

French term, meaning "burnt"—a dish with a crisp topping of caramelized sugar.

Chine

To cut through the rib bones of a roast (usually lamb or pork) close to the backbone or spine, or to remove the backbone from a rib roast or rack of meat, to make the meat easier to carve.

Coulis

A smooth sauce (of pouring consistency) made by puréeing raw or cooked fruit or cooked vegetables.

Cure

Preserve meat, poultry, or fish by smoking, drying or salting. Curing also adds flavor to food.

Deglaze

To heat liquid, such as stock, water, or wine, with the juices and sediment left in a pan after roasting or frying meat or vegetables, stirring and scraping until the sediment has combined with the liquid to make a sauce or gravy.

Disgorge/Degorge

To draw out moisture, extract bitter juices, or remove impurities from food by one of two methods: sprinkling the food with salt and letting it stand, then rinsing and drying it before cooking (for example, eggplants and cucumbers); or soaking the food in water before cooking (for example, meat, offal, fish).

En croûte

Term used to describe food such as fish, meat, or fruit that is wrapped in pastry before baking.

En papillote

Food that is sealed and baked in a parcel of baking paper or foil. The cooked dish is served from the parcel.

Flambé

To add an alcoholic spirit such as brandy, rum, or whisky to a dish, and then ignite it to burn off the alcohol and add flavor.

Florentine

A savory dish (usually fish or eggs) served with, or containing, spinach, and often cheese sauce.

Fold in

To combine a whisked or creamed mixture by gently cutting into it using a large metal spoon or plastic spatula, to keep as much air as possible in the mixture.

Ganache

A very rich mixture of melted chocolate and cream, which is used as a filling or coating for cakes, pastries, desserts, and so on.

Infuse

To impart flavor into a liquid by adding ingredients such as a vanilla bean, spices, or herbs. The infused liquid is often heated, then left to stand and strained before use.

Julienne

Vegetables, fruit, or citrus zest cut into very fine "matchstick" strips.

Lard

To insert, or thread small strips (lardons) of fat or bacon through the flesh of lean meat, game birds, and poultry using a larding needle, to add succulence and flavor to the meat during roasting.

Liaison

Ingredients used to thicken or bind soups or sauces. Egg yolks, cream, blood, or a combination of ingredients such as flour and water or cream and egg yolks are typical liaisons.

Macerate

To soak raw or dried foods such as fruit in a liquid, such as alcohol or sugar syrup, to soften and flavor the food.

Marinate

To soak or treat raw meat, poultry, or fish in a paste or sauce (usually including oil, wine, lemon juice or vinegar, and other flavorings) to tenderize, flavor, and add moisture.

Pare

To peel thinly the skin or zest from fruit or vegetables.

Punch down

To deflate risen yeast dough, in order to disperse the gases created by the fermentation process throughout the dough, to ensure an even texture.

Reduce/Reduction

To fast-boil a stock, sauce, or gravy in an uncovered pan, so the liquid reduces to a fraction of its original volume. The reduction becomes thicker and its flavor more concentrated.

Roux

A mixture of equal amounts of fat (usually butter) and flour cooked together (to different degrees of color) and used to thicken liquids to make sauces or soups.

Rub in

Incorporate fat into flour and other dry ingredients by rubbing the ingredients together using your fingertips, until the mixture resembles breadcrumbs. This creates a short texture used in some pastry, scone, cake, and shortbread recipes.

Sauté

To shallow-fry food in hot melted fat in an uncovered pan over high heat, shaking the pan or tossing the food continuously, until browned all over.

Scald

To pour boiling water over fruit such as tomatoes or peaches to loosen skins. Also, to heat a liquid such as milk until it is just below boiling point.

Seal/Sear

To brown meat rapidly all over in hot melted fat before further cooking, to seal in the juices and give it flavor and color.

Steep

To soak food in warm or cold liquid to soften it, to absorb the flavors of the liquid (as from a marinade), or to draw out strong flavors or salt from the food.

Sweat

To cook food, typically sliced or chopped vegetables, gently in a little melted fat or stock, in a covered pan, until the food is soft but not colored or browned.

Temper

To heat then cool chocolate to specific temperatures, to make it easier to use and to produce a glossy finish when it sets.

Truss

To tie or skewer poultry, game birds, or boned joints of meat into a neat shape before cooking.

index

picture credits

Photography by

Peter Cassidy
Pages 1, 13 below, 15 right, 17, 18, 20, 21, 24, 25, 29, 35, 42, 44, 55, 79

Martin Brigdale
Pages 2, 23, 33 above, 34, 43, 49, 52, 53, 66, 67, 68, 69, 84, 85 above

William Lingwood
Pages 11, 27 both, 37 below, 51, 54, 60 above, 61, 65, 74 above, 75

Patrice de Villiers
Pages 14, 16, 30, 32 both, 33 below, 70, 71, 74 below

Nicki Dowey
Pages 28 below, 31, 57, 60 below

Tara Fisher
Pages 5, 8, 9, 81

Richard Jung
Pages 6, 73, 76, 82

Craig Roberston
Pages 13 above, 15 left, 46, 47

Debi Treloar
Pages 3, 41, 77, 87

Ian Wallace
Pages 4, 22 below, 48

Jeremy Hopley
Pages 62 below, 63

Jason Lowe
Pages 28 above, 62 above

Noel Murphy
Pages 38, 45

Alan Williams
Pages 37 above, 85 below

Caroline Arber
Page 12

Christopher Drake
Endpapers

Chris Everard
Page 7

James Merrell
Page 22 above

David Munns
Page 36

Peter Myers
Page 26

William Reavell
Page 83

acknowledgments

I would like to thank Alison Starling at Ryland Peters & Small for approaching me and asking me to write this book, and for her continued support throughout this project. I would also like to thank Clare Double for her comprehensive and thorough editing, and Paul Tilby for his creative design. Finally, my special thanks go to my husband, Robbie, for his ongoing support and encouragement with this book.